# I Have Your Number: A Funny Guide to Why People Drive You Nuts

Self-Discovery for People Who Hate
Self-Help Books
Dating and Relationship Edition

Debra Zachau

# Table of Contents

1

2

3

4

5

6

7

8

9

# 11

# 22

# 33

# 44

# 55

*I Have Your Number*

I Have Your Number
A Funny Guide To Why People Drive You Nuts
Self-Discovery For People Who Hate Self-Help Books
Published By Taking Fight Publishing
Oceanside, California, U.S.A.

Zachau, Debra
I Have Your Number

Library Of Congress Control Number: LCCN 2025918882
ISBN: (Paperback) 978-1-7323426-6-8 (E Book) 978-1-7323426-7-5
ISBN: (Audiobook) 978-1-7323426-8-2

Books / Self Help / Relationships / Dating
Books / Self Help / Transformational Self Help
Books / Religion & Spirituality / New Age Spirituality / Divination / Numerology
Books / Humor & Entertainment / Humor / Love Sex & Marriage

Quantity Purchases: Schools, Companies, Professional Groups, Clubs, And Other Organizations May Qualify For Special Terms When Ordering Quantities Of This Title.
For Information, Email Info@Takingflightpublishing.Com

# Special Thanks:

Editor: Denise Waldrep

Cover Design: Qurat Z (Fiverr)

Book Formatting Muzammil Hayat (Fiverr)

Beta Readers:

Latit Stalb @AstrologyVibrations

Kayleigh Gordon @ThanksHolySpirit

Valerie Bradshaw @illuminationPortal

Sara @hibiscushealings

Gerald, @TarotStache

*"At any one time,
you are someone's teacher or
student. The trouble begins when
you assume which one you are".*
*-Debra Zachau*

# Author's Note

Before we go too far, I want to pause and tell you why this book may sound different than other numerology guides you've read. I didn't just memorize the traditional traits of Life Path numbers and repeat them back to you; I tested them. Over years of coaching and more than 11,000 client sessions, I've asked questions, taken notes, and compared what's written in the books to how these numbers actually showed up in real life. Spoiler: sometimes the archetypes matched beautifully, and sometimes they were so off-base I had to laugh. (And then rewrite them.)

When I added numerology into my coaching business, I wasn't looking for parlor tricks; I wanted something practical that could help me serve others well. And it did. It sharpened my accuracy in remarkable ways. Knowing someone's Life Path number gave me the right words at the right time. I often say: if someone was standing on a bridge ready to jump, and you knew their Life Path number, you would know precisely what to say to reach them in that moment.

That's not just a metaphor. Once, after a session with a client, he admitted to my manager the next day that he had already prepared the rope and chair to end his life if the session with me didn't go well. Because of what I've learned by refining numerology through countless real conversations, I was able to mirror back to him the traits that made him remarkable and unique in this world. And he changed his mind. He lived. I never forgot that moment. It's why I take this work so seriously, even though I deliver it here with humor and levity.

And this is a learnable skill! It has nothing to do with how much intuition a person has. It's math and some good information put together so you can be a better partner, co-worker, friend, and family member. In other words, create an easier life with less guesswork.

So yes, this book is lighthearted, irreverent, and full of adult humor, but don't mistake that for trivial. Behind the jokes, I'm dead serious about the power of self-discovery and numerology's ability to explain why people do what they do. Once you understand the "why," you can see what's a natural quirk and what's negotiable. And once you know that, life becomes easier to navigate, relationships smoother, compassion easier, and patience more possible. That's the spirit in which I've written this book: field-tested insights mixed with real-life levity. Because if we can laugh at ourselves while learning who we are, and why we drive each other crazy, maybe we'll also find a way to love each other better.

# Introduction: Love by the Numbers (But Not by the Rules)

Let's get relationships straight from the very beginning: Just because someone somewhere said your numbers don't match your soulmates, doesn't mean you have to break up, pack your things, and start over with someone who meditates at the same frequency as your number. I mean, have you ever met two "perfectly matched" people who couldn't stand each other after a long car ride? Yeah, I know, right? There is so much more to a person than a single number. While numerology gives us helpful clues, it's not a cosmic sentence or a relationship death certificate. I've read for countless couples who, by the numbers, should have had trouble, but didn't. And I've read for a few that looked great on paper, but couldn't agree on what pizza to order. So, what's the difference?

*Awareness.*

When you understand someone's sensitivities and strengths, you gain the power to reflect back their best selves. And everyone likes that, especially when we forget what our best self even looks like. This book will help you see not only the gifts your partner brings into your life, but also the lessons they're learning in this lifetime. It gives you tools to support their growth... or sabotage them spectacularly, because you'll know precisely what their emotional kryptonite is. (*Please don't do that.*)

The most attractive trait anyone can have, whether you're a friend, partner, spouse, teacher, or parent, is the awareness of what lights someone up… and what shuts them down. When you know someone's joy buttons and their sad triggers, and you act with kindness and intention, it changes everything. Understanding the numbers gives you a shortcut to that kind of insight. So, what does this kind of relationship look like?

The *"get to know your person better so you don't lose your mind during Mercury retrograde"* kind.

The *"ohhhh, that's why he panics when I cry"* kind.

The *"I should probably stop pushing that button"* kind.

You'll laugh. You'll cringe (at yourself). You'll learn things you didn't know you needed to know. So please, use this information with kindness. With curiosity. And with an occasional eye roll, because let's be honest, relationships are weird and messy and beautiful and baffling: (did I say messy?). And the more tools we have to love each other better, the better off we all are.

## So… Why Are You Like This? (And Why is Everyone Else so Annoying?)

Let's be honest: people are confusing, including you. Why did your ex-ghost you after you introduced them to your crystal collection?

Why does your coworker chew like a goat but still get promoted?

Why do you feel spiritually allergic to group projects?

Why does your cousin Greg constantly start businesses... and then abandon them to "find himself in Aruba"?

Why is your partner emotionally allergic to hugs, but cries during car commercials?

Why do you get irrationally angry when someone walks too slowly in front of you at the grocery store?

Why do you feel like you're meant for something bigger, but also need a nap, like... all the time?

The answer to all of these may not be trauma. (Although let's be honest, it's partially trauma.)

You will understand why when you understand Life Path numbers.

Numerology is the ancient study of numbers and their cosmic meanings, kind of like astrology's nerdy, math-obsessed sibling who actually shows up on time. The Life Path number is its bold, bossy centerpiece on the table of life. (I know, I went too far on that one. Sorry.)

This number, derived only from your full date of birth, is like your soul's job description for this lifetime. It's your theme, your vibe, your energetic "why." It's the number that whispers, "You're here to lead," or, "You're here to heal," or, "You're here to learn patience", (which is hilarious because you have none).

Your number doesn't care about your job title, your rising sign, or how many crystals you've charged under the full moon. It's your spiritual contract with the universe, signed in invisible ink at birth, kind of like the Terms & Conditions of your soul (except this time, you're actually going to read it, if you're smart). And no, you don't have to be a math whiz. In fact, this book only talks about your Life Path number, which is derived by adding up your birthday, one number at a time. Easy Peezy.

You just need to be curious, slightly open to magic, and willing to admit that maybe, just maybe, you've been making life harder than it has to be. No need to decode your name or learn the alphabet-to-number chart (we're skipping that part). In this book, we're keeping it simple and focused:

**One number. One Life Path. One enlightening (and occasionally hilarious) journey.**

So, grab a calculator (or don't, it's just addition), and get ready to discover:

Why you're bold and bossy (and mildly stressed), hello Life Path 1 and 4.

Why your chill friend who says "the universe will provide" is probably a 7.

Why your cousin, who keeps buying group planners but never uses them, is almost definitely a 5.

How about that co-worker whose desk is always neat and tidy, enjoys structured routines, and is always the sensible one? She comes by it naturally, Miss. 4 (written with a sneer...I'm a disorganized 11).

## What Can Numerology Actually Do for You?

Glad you asked. Here's a breakdown:

**Personality profiling without the therapy bill:**

Each number has its own energy, like astrological signs, but it is less likely to argue about Mercury always being in retrograde. Your numbers reveal things like whether you're naturally ambitious or just really good at looking busy. (Spoiler: if you're a 1, you're both.)

**Life Path analysis: Your soul's GPS.**

Your number is your soul's job title in this lifetime. It's like being handed your cosmic marching orders, except instead of "Assistant Regional Manager," it's something cooler, like "Creative Warrior," "Master Healer," or "Determined-but-Slightly-Bossy Visionary." (Hi, again, 1. You too 4.)

It tells you what lessons you're here to learn, what obstacles will trip you up (again and again), and what kind of life will leave you feeling fulfilled.

**Relationship intel (AKA: Why you and Todd keep fighting over the dishwasher?)**

Numerology is the nosy friend who can't help but analyze every couple it meets and is usually right. By comparing your numbers with someone else's, you'll see where you align, where you clash, and whether you're destined for greatness… or at least fewer passive-aggressive texts.

**Career clarity:** Yes, this book is about relationships, but it's also a cheat sheet for championing the people you love. It helps you spot what your partner's naturally good at, which comes in very handy when they're stuck in an "I don't know what I want to do with my life" spiral. You'll have insights they didn't even know they needed, like a cool career coach disguised as a loving partner. Numerology can help with suggestions. Based on your core numbers, you'll uncover the type of work that makes you, your partner, and your friends feel alive.

**Spiritual growth for the chronically curious:**

Beyond career and compatibility, numerology offers deep insights into your soul's journey. It helps you align with your higher self, heal old patterns, and finally understand why you choke up during those dog food commercials. (I know that pup looks like your childhood best friend, Max, when he was young. Sorry to bring it up again.)

**Personality decoder:**

Ever feel like you're a mix of Type A, free spirit, and emotionally frozen motivational speaker? That's not a glitch, it's your Life Path showing up in weird and wonderful ways. This number reveals your natural strengths, weaknesses, and the inner monologue you didn't even know you were broadcasting to the world.

**Why you're attracted to (and irritated by) certain people:**

Life Path compatibility is real, and very helpful when trying to understand why your relationship feels like a kind of boot camp or why your best friend drives you nuts but gets you better than anyone else.

**Life lessons you can't seem to escape:**

That annoying pattern that keeps coming up over and over again? Your number might be the reason you keep dating emotionally unavailable poets or feel like you're constantly trusting people who keep turning out to be low-down cheatin' daddies.

**Why you work the way you do:**

Whether you're a workaholic with a wall-sized to-do board for productivity or someone who needs a three-day nap after every Zoom call (I'm raising my hand on this one), your number can explain your approach to goals, structure, and finding meaning in what you do.

You'll also meet your Master Numbers, double digits with double the intensity (and sometimes double the drama). These power players (11, 22, 33, 44, and 55) bring elevated missions, spiritual downloads, and occasional existential panic. It's fine. We'll walk through it together.

Wait... Is this actually scientific?

Well, no. And also... kind of.

Numerology isn't science in the lab-coat-and-goggles sense. But it is based on mathematics, pattern recognition, and centuries of observation. There's even a niche field called numerological physics that explores how number patterns might reflect natural laws. And honestly, when a number system designed in ancient Greece can explain your attachment issues better than your therapist, who needs a peer-reviewed journal?

## Why This Book is Different?

This book doesn't go into name-based destiny numbers, expression numbers, or the metaphysical meaning of how many vowels are in your dog's name. We're sticking to the basics, the birthdate-based Life Path number, because:

It's accurate.

It's consistent.

It's easy to calculate.

And frankly, it's freakin' crazy how much it explains about people.

So, buckle up, grab your birthday (no ID needed), and let's dive into the cosmic blueprint you've been carrying around since birth.

## First, a Little History, Pythagorean vs. Chaldean: A Brief but Juicy Side Note.

There are two major schools of thought regarding numerology:

Chaldean, which is sound-based and mysterious and great if you're into ancient codes and shadowy vibes.

Pythagorean, which is number-based and cleanly mathematical, like if Socrates taught a geometry class with spiritual undertones.

This book uses the Pythagorean system because it's:

Easier to calculate (you can do it on a napkin).

I've discovered it's more consistent with personality patterns.

Rich with information about Master Numbers (which the Chaldean system barely glances at, (rude). No shade meant.

The Pythagorean system includes the 9 and also addresses the unique pressures of the master numbers. (If, after adding up your birthdate, you reach a double-digit number, such as 11, 22, 33, 44, 55, you do not reduce it to one digit. (I know, I know, that's a tricky part about adding the numbers.) Master numbers bring more information as well as insight into the unique challenges of those big, phat double-digit numbers. Plus, Pythagorean numerology lets you geek out on how the number itself behaves, which tells us way more about you than any birthstone ever could.

**So, what now?**

In the chapters ahead, we're going to break down each Life Path number in regard to relationships, starting with the glorious (and occasionally high-strung) Life Path 1.

You'll laugh. You'll nod. You'll probably say, "Oh my god, that's so me."

Whether you're a 1 blazing your own trail or a 7 who just wants to be left alone in peace and pajamas, there's something here for everyone.

Let's unlock the math of your soul.

# Your Life Path Number: How to Calculate it (Without Summoning Math Trauma or Breaking the Universe)

Okay, deep breath. It's time to do math. But friendly math.

This is not the kind of math that made you cry in 9th-grade geometry. This is soul math. Cosmic math. Math with meaning. And trust me, it's worth it, because your number is like your personal instruction manual for being human.

**The easy way that's also the correct way, (Take that, overcomplicators!)**

So here we are, ready to uncover the one number that secretly explains everything about you, your ambitions, your weird dating patterns, your allergy to group texts, and your slightly unhinged need to be 15 minutes early to everything.

Calculating it does not require an abacus, a crystal grid, or breaking your birth date into chunks like some numerologists insist on doing. We're not baking a spiritual layer cake here; we're just adding numbers, one at a time, the way nature (and the cosmos) intended. (Again, no shade on those who like to add the chunky way.)

**Now, before we get into it, let's clear up one very important thing:**

There is a right way and a complicated way to do this.

And yes, numerology cares. Your soul cares. I care.

So, let's do it the right way, not the chop it up then slap-it-all-together-like-a-leftover-dinner way.

**Step 1: Write down your full birth date (in numbers).**

Let's say your birthday is May 5, 1990. That's:

5 / 5 / 1990

Now, just ignore the slashes and start adding like your soul depends on it. Yes, it's that easy…

**Step 2: Add all the digits together.**

So, from our example:

$5 + 5 + 1 + 9 + 9 + 0 = 29$

Then reduce the 29 by adding:

$2 + 9 = 11$

**BOOM**. You've got a Master Number. Stop there. Frame it. Embroider it on a pillow. Do not reduce it further.

But if your number isn't 11, 22, 33, 44, or 55 (a.k.a. numerology's really odd family that lives down the block, you walk by fast, avoiding eye contact), then go ahead and reduce again until you get a single-digit number between 1 and 9.

**Another example: 4/25/1999.**

Write it as:

$4 + 2 + 5 + 1 + 9 + 9 + 9 = 39$

Then reduce the 39 by adding the two numbers together:

$3 + 9 = 12$

Then again to reach a single digit number:

$1 + 2 = 3$

So, this person's Life Path number is 3. A natural-born communicator, storyteller, and person most likely to accidentally overshare in an elevator.

**Example with history: 9/11/2001.**

Yep, we're going there, but gently.

$9 + 1 + 1 + 2 + 0 + 0 + 1 = 14$

Reduce again, like before: $1 + 4 = 5$

Number 5 represents the energy of that day, the number of change. Fast, sometimes shocking, always transformational.

On that day, the energy of the 5 was undeniable. But even deeper are the two numbers that created it:

The 1, in shadow, brings domination, intolerance, and ruthless control.

The 4, when unbalanced, can turn into rigid dogma, fear, and authoritarianism.

Together, this energy cracked something open on a global level. Remember the *people, NOT the numbers*, created that storm. A date that shocked the world and marked a permanent shift in the collective experience.

Numerology doesn't explain away pain. But it gives language to the unseen forces underneath events, so we can understand them, heal from them, and maybe, just maybe, learn through them.

**To recap the method of calculating.**

Add every single digit in your birthdate one right after the other. Keep going until you get a single digit (unless it's a Master Number). That's it. No slicing, no reducing separate parts if only on a Tuesday. Simple and fun. Don't overthink the calculations. The numbers are watching. (Not in a creepy way, more like a spiritually passive-aggressive way that makes your intuition itch.)

Do a little victory dance, you now know your Life Path number.

**Make a list, and blow your mind! (A fun way to use this book like a spy tool.)**

Okay, now that you've added up your birthday (hooray, you did math!), it's time to make things personal. And slightly nosy.

Here's a simple but addictive exercise:

After calculating your number, calculate the birthdays of everyone around you. I'm serious. Everyone. Start with your inner circle and spiral outward like a curious, slightly mystical detective.

Your assignment (A.K.A. your secret numerology recon mission):

List the birthdays of your family members. This includes the ones you like and the ones who show up to Thanksgiving with unsolicited opinions. Yes, even Cousin Chad. Especially Cousin Chad.

Add in your best friend(s). You already share memes and trauma. Why not also share your number? Don't forget that one friend you secretly admire but can't help but compete with. If your frenemy turns out to be an 8 and you're a 2... things are going to click really fast, like in a good way.

Toss in your boss, your favorite (or least favorite) coworker, your ex, and your barista if you know their birthday. Because sometimes enlightenment looks like realizing your team lead is a 4, and now you finally understand why she color-codes everything, to keep everyone organized. And of course... that one celebrity you've followed forever.

If you've spent the last 10 years emotionally invested in an actor, pop star, or reality TV villain, you deserve to know what makes them tick. Don't forget the famous figures in history. Wait until you look up Einstein, Volodymyr Zelenskyy, Alexei Navalny, and don't forget Ben Franklin, whom I find to be a quirky, brilliant polymath who traveled all over the world. (Spoiler...Life Path 5 of course).

**Why bother?**

Because once you start reading each Life Path personality, you'll suddenly understand:

Why your mom cries over everything (hello, 2).

Why does your brother talk like he's constantly delivering a keynote speech, (1 or 8).

Why your co-worker's Slack messages read like poetry (I see you, 3).

Why your ex disappeared mid-conversation and reemerged two years later with a van and a podcast (ahem, 5).

Why your favorite celebrity gives off wounded healer vibes (shoutout to all the 9s).

You'll laugh. You'll gasp. You'll text someone something like, "OH MY GOD THIS IS SO YOU."

**Or, reverse engineer the process...**

As you read through the different personality traits assigned to each number, don't be surprised if a specific person pops into your head. That's not a coincidence, it's your intuition whispering, "Yep, this explains a lot."

As you read the words, a memory, person, or event will pop into your mind, and you may feel compelled to look up their birthday or event date. Do it! You will finally understand why your Uncle Carl always spins a simple story into an epic diatribe of action and adventure. Why your co-worker moves between mirror selfies and mumbling disparagingly about her eyebrows. When numerology clicks, it clicks, like the last satisfying piece of a jigsaw puzzle that finally makes the whole picture clear.

And how about Wilbur and Orville Wright making such a great team? (Wilbur, April 16, 1867, and Orville, August 19, 1871). Add them up. So cool. Ah, Spoiler: Opposites that understand and accept each other's genius (commonly known as quirks) can absolutely make history.

**A few notes before you spiral:**

Don't weaponize this information.

"Yeah, I knew you were a 4, you emotional glacier!" *is not an appropriate use of this knowledge.* Use it to deepen your understanding, not fuel your revenge arc. This isn't a magic trick, but it is a mirror. And sometimes? A really helpful decoder ring.

Feel free to scribble down your findings in the margins. This book is meant to be used. Highlight, underline, and make lists in the back. Doodle hearts around your Life Path soulmate. Draw lightning bolts next to your villain's origin story. (I won't judge). Knowing someone's Life Path number is like getting a sneak peek at their emotional operating system. Once you see the patterns, it's hard not to start connecting the dots.

So go ahead, be nosy, be curious, be that person who pulls out a calculator at brunch and says, "I know your birthday. You're a 7, aren't you?" You'll be surprised how often you're right. You'll become the person who suddenly *gets* everyone. When in need, you will have the right combination of words to help and heal others, and people will think you have a new superpower.

# Quick Peek: Your Life Path Personality, Summed Up

Before I jump into the deep end of each number, let's take a quick detour to acknowledge something important:

Yes, people are messy. Complex. Ever-changing. And no, your Life Path number is not the reason to ghost people, cancel plans last minute, or sob at nature documentaries. Numerology reveals your core personality blueprint, the part of you that existed before emotional baggage, childhood conditioning, and the questionable decision to date that one person who "just needed a place to stay for a while." It describes your natural tendencies before the world piled on expectations, guilt, and glittery Instagram advice.

So, if you read something that sounds... less than flattering? Don't panic. It's not an accusation; it's a range of possibilities. You're human. You've probably made a few shady choices. But that doesn't mean you're doomed to be a boundary-ignoring love tornado or a micromanaging spreadsheet tyrant. It just means you've "got range".

This list is your cheat sheet to understanding yourself and others at a glance. It's especially helpful when dating, dealing with relatives, hiring assistants, or trying to figure out why your new friend says she's "definitely not mad" but keeps blinking aggressively.

## Life Path quick peek: Tiny descriptions, big personality clues.

1. Comfortable standing alone, fiercely individualistic, pivots faster than most people make coffee. ("I am.")

2. Loves teamwork and tenderness but occasionally forgets where their own needs are. ("We are.")

3. A walking Pinterest board of creativity, charm, and mild chaos. Expressive and entertaining. ("I create.")

4. The steady builder. Plans, structure, systems, and suspicious side-eyes at your "spontaneous road trip." ("I (we) build.")

5. Freedom-chasing, suitcase-packing, commitment-avoiding adventure junkie. Gets bored easily. ("I explore.")

6. Nurturer, harmonizer, accidental martyr. Just wants everyone to eat, love, and use coasters. ("I support.")

7. Deep thinker, cosmic detective, solitude-loving sage who tries to tolerate small talk. ("I believe.")

8. Power suit energy. Natural leader, money magnet, sometimes forgets they have emotions. ("I lead.")

9. Old soul. Legacy vibes. Might cry over a tree, but has a deeply strategic mind. ("I teach.")

11. Enlightenment on legs. Feels everything, questions everything, beams with potential. ("I illuminate.")

22. The ultimate builder of big ideas. Collaborator, connector, often running five communities at once. ("We network & build.")

33. The cosmic artist. Healer, creator, emotional sponge. Brings beauty into form. ("I bring into being.")

44. Infrastructure meets compassion. Builder of safe spaces and sustainable systems. ("I build and protect.")

55. Disruptor of outdated systems. Pushes buttons and asks, "But what if everything could be better?" ("I question and authenticate.")

# Life Path 1: The Trailblazing Maverick with a Mild God Complex (But in a Cute Way)

Let's face it: if a 1 were a person in your friend group, they'd be the one with the vision board, a five-year plan, and a suspiciously expensive pen they definitely didn't buy on sale. 1's are the trailblazers of numerology, the go-getters, the pioneers, the human equivalent of a triple-shot espresso with a dash of Michael Jordan, Ketanji Brown Jackson level ambition.

These people are born with the energetic equivalent of an "I got this" tattoo stamped on their soul. They are so independent, you could lock them in a room with a Rubik's cube, a toothpick, and a dream, and they'd MacGyver their way into inventing a new branch of science. But before we go pinning medals on their chest, let's take a closer look at what makes the mighty 1 tick (and tick off others, sometimes because, let's be honest, their intensity can be a lot).

**The spark plug of the zodiac (Oops, wrong system, but still applies).**

1s are the initiators of the numerological world. Think of them as the flint that sparks the fire or, if you prefer a modern metaphor, the person who decides to launch a business in the middle of a recession because they had a "gut feeling" and a "really good logo." These are the ones who don't wait to be picked; they pick themselves, thank you very much. They're action-oriented, leadership-prone, and allergic to the words "group project." Hand them a clipboard and they'll run the meeting. Hand them a sword and they'll declare themselves the general. Hand them a compliment, and they'll silently agree that it was well-earned.

Their motto? "If I want it done right, I'll do it myself." This explains why 1s often wake up at 2:00 a.m. to re-do a task that someone else did just fine.

1 Life Path people are innately confident, and if they ever doubt themselves, they will not show it. They might be internally crumbling like gluten-free cake under pressure, but on the outside? Cool as a cucumber with a master plan and backup snacks. Their gift is decisive action. While other people are still overthinking whether they should start a blog, and first check to see if the topic is trending, and the best keywords to use, a 1 has

written 10 posts, built a website, launched a merch line, and is negotiating a podcast sponsorship with their cat as a co-host.

Their curse? They don't always ask for help. They think they're being strong and self-sufficient, but their friends are over there like, "You could have just texted me, Linda. I own a moving van." To a 1, asking for help feels like failure. But to everyone else, it just looks like a person carrying an entire couch up the stairs alone… backwards… in the rain… with a dislocated sense of teamwork.

When it comes to relationships, romantic or platonic, 1s are intense, loyal, and occasionally a bit of a handful (but a lovable one, like a golden retriever that just must lead the pack). They value partners who are strong, capable, and low drama. You know, like themselves, if you ask them. (Others may gently disagree.)

Their idea of a great date? Conquering a hiking trail, launching a joint business, or working out at 6 a.m. while discussing long-term goals and the merits of oat milk. They'll adore you if you're confident. They'll ignore you if you're clingy. And they'll absolutely ghost you if you don't believe in their dream to start a motivational YouTube channel for the misunderstood iguana.

Love with a 1 is a whirlwind, equal parts inspiration, ambition, and self-improvement YouTube vibes. Don't take it personally if they forget your anniversary; they were probably busy scaling their personal Everest.

## The Dating and Flirt Style of a Life Path 1: Confidence, Commitment, and Just a Dash of Control Issues.

Ah, a 1 in love. Dating one is like getting swept up in a motivational montage; you'll feel inspired, slightly exhausted, and suddenly find yourself optimizing your morning routine. These individuals don't just date; they strategize romance. First dates are treated like job interviews (minus the resume, plus a PowerPoint in their head titled "Why I'd be an excellent partner"). You won't get vague texts or passive flirting here, nope, they come in hot with direct eye contact, confident moves, and possibly an outline of where this relationship is going by dessert.

They radiate confidence. It's not even something they try to do; it just leaks out of them like expensive cologne mixed with ambition. You'll know they're into you because they tell you. Directly. Probably with a well-timed compliment and a firm handshake that says, "I'm interviewing you for the position of lifelong co-star." Don't expect vague hints or subtlety. If a 1 wants you, you'll know. If they don't, you'll also know. Quickly. It's a gift. And a curse.

1s don't "hang out." They initiate. They've already picked the restaurant, confirmed the reservation, googled what place makes your favorite dessert, and subtly dropped hints that they might change your life. Whether it's a surprise weekend getaway or an intense conversation about your 5-year goals, dating them feels like being drafted into a motivational novel. They'll take the lead, open the door, and possibly challenge you to a productivity contest. And when they fall? They fall hard. But don't mistake their intensity for clinginess. It's more like, "I love you deeply, but I also have a call at 6 a.m. tomorrow. Let's be efficient."

## Dating and Flirt Style of a 1: Masculine Edition

A 1 man dates with purpose. He's not here to "see where it goes", he knows where it's going, and he'd like you to keep up. Confident, direct, and naturally independent, he leads in both conversation and plans, often showing up with reservations already made and a backup plan just in case. He's not flashy, he's focused. This is the guy who shows you he's interested by creating space for you in a life that's already in motion. He's drawn to strong partners but will try not to compete; he respects individuality but needs to feel trusted in his role. Underneath the ambition? A deep desire to protect, provide, and build something real. He doesn't waste time, and if he's all in, you'll never have to wonder.

**The Aloof Factor: "I like you. I'm just also very busy being iconic."**

Yes, they're charming and charismatic, but sometimes they come off a little… emotionally MIA. That's not because they don't care, it's just that their brain is busy winning at 42 other things simultaneously. While you're waiting for a text back, they might be rewriting their goal list or finishing a PowerPoint for a million-dollar deal. Give them a minute. Or an hour. Once they remember they're not dating a whiteboard calendar, they'll show up with intense eye contact and a plan for your shared future.

**Passion Level: 100% Fire Emoji.**

1s are passionate, loyal, and sometimes intense to the point of needing to be unplugged and restarted. But if you like your romance with a bit of heat, a little drama, and a lot of "we can do anything together," then you're in luck. They'll hype you up like your own personal cheer squad, but don't expect cuddly coasting. They love the climb. They love ambition. And if you have your own passions? Even better. Just know that if you bring a weak dream to the table, they'll try to upgrade it into a six-figure business.

**The Challenge: Their standards are so high that birds hit them in flight.**

1s are perfectionists with dating standards that range from "must be emotionally mature" to "should also be fluent in five love languages and mildly psychic." They want it all: chemistry, ambition, personal growth, a shared love of efficiency. And when reality doesn't match their idealized vision? Prepare for a minor existential crisis, followed by a two-hour journal session and a breakup letter. They're not afraid to be single if it means holding out for a partner who gets it. And by "gets it," I mean "understands that we're building an empire here, not just watching Netflix."

Once you're in with a 1, it's game on. They're loyal, devoted, and wildly supportive. You'll feel like you're dating a life coach, business partner, and occasional drill sergeant all wrapped into one very goal-oriented human. They'll remember your dreams, push you to achieve them, and text inspirational quotes at 6:30 a.m. Whether it's love or legacy, they don't half-do anything.

But here's the catch: don't get too comfortable. The moment they sense you're not growing, they'll start "casually suggesting" improvement plans. If you're not into becoming your best self, this may not be your ride. They won't ghost you unless you ghost your own potential. Their version of romance isn't always candlelit dinners and love songs. It's "I believe in you so much I bought you a planner." If you can handle a love story that comes with quarterly check-ins and passion-fueled pep talks, you're in for one of the most inspiring, dynamic relationships of your life.

**So, you've fallen for a 1?** Congratulations, you may be dating a future cult leader (of the inspirational kind). To help you keep up with their intensity and keep your sanity, here's your essential cheat sheet.

**DO:**

**Do applaud their drive.** They just launched a podcast, opened an Etsy shop, and joined a leadership mastermind group in the same week. Clap. Loudly. They thrive on validation and coffee-fueled momentum.

**Do let them take the lead, at least sometimes.** They'll insist on planning your entire anniversary weekend. Let them. Just nod enthusiastically and pretend you didn't already reserve a table. They need this.

**Do have your own dreams.** A 1 doesn't want a sidekick; they want a partner with equal ambition. If your idea of romance is sitting close to each other on the couch for three years, this may not be your movie.

**Do speak their language.** Confidence. Directness. Progress. Words like "someday" or "maybe" give them emotional hives. Say what you mean, show up on time, and never respond "idk" when they ask where the relationship is going.

**DON'T:**

**Don't be wishy washy.** They'll respect you more for saying "I disagree" than for saying "Whatever you want." Spinelessness makes their third eye, the visionary part of them. Glitch out.

**Don't interrupt their flow.** If they're in "the zone," back away... slowly. 1s are friendly creatures, but if you interrupt their productivity, you will get that "I'm smiling but dying inside" stare.

**Don't take it personally if they're blunt.** They don't mean to sound like your overly assertive boss. It's just how they love: direct, intense, and occasionally with bullet points.

**Emergency affirmations for dating a 1:** If you're ever overwhelmed by their ambition, intensity, or third unsolicited vision board, repeat after me:

"Just because they're confident doesn't mean I'm underachieving."

"They love me. They just also love plans, goals, and winning."

"I am not a project. I am a partner."

"It's okay if I don't know my five-year plan. I'll fake it till I do."

"I will not take it personally if they rearrange my pantry for optimal efficiency."

Love a 1 and you'll never be bored. You'll be challenged, encouraged, and occasionally exhausted, but you'll also be wildly inspired. They're here to help you rise... but maybe set some gentle boundaries from the very beginning, just sayin'.

## Spotting a 1 in the Wild: Standing Tall (Like They Own the Building).

You'll rarely catch a 1 slouching. They carry themselves like they've just been elected president of something important, even if it's just the carpool. Their posture says, "I believe in myself. You should too." And honestly? You kind of do.

**Unapologetic eye contact. Direct. Intentional. Laser-beam-y.**

A 1 will look you straight in the eyes and ask you what your five-year plan is before you've even finished your coffee. They're not trying to intimidate (okay, sometimes they are), they just don't believe in small talk or wasted moments.

**Firm handshake (Sometimes a little too firm).**

They shake hands like they're closing a deal, even if you're just meeting at a farmer's market. It's not aggressive, it's just... decisive. You'll know if you're talking to a 1 by how much your fingers tingle afterward.

**Assertive gestures. Chop. Point. Slice. Air karate.**

1s use their hands like exclamation marks. When they're passionate (which is always), expect sharp gestures, purposeful motion, and the occasional palm-down "let me finish" movement. They walk like they're late for a keynote speech, even when they're just going to the kitchen. You'll never catch a 1 meandering. Their pace says, "I have goals, and one of them is arriving three minutes earlier than you."

**They take up space.**

Sitting with arms draped wide, standing with feet planted confidently apart, or accidentally dominating a conversation, a 1's physical presence is felt. They're not trying to dominate; they're just built to lead. And they figure the room will adjust.

## Spiritual Lessons for a 1:

The soul of a 1 came here to learn what it means to trust its own voice, even when it's the only one in the room. This path is all about developing courage, independence, and self-leadership without tipping into lonely, controlling, or "I'll just do it myself because no one else gets it" territory. 1s are meant to carve their own way, yes, but they're also here to learn that being first doesn't mean going it alone. Spirit is teaching them how to take the lead without stepping on toes, to stand tall without steamrolling, and to value collaboration without losing their originality. It's a lifetime of learning to be bold without being brittle. When they tune into their higher self, 1s realize that true power doesn't always come from being the loudest voice, but from being the clearest one.

**From a Life Path 1's perspective. Their perfect partner:**

Great Match. Easy flow, natural understanding; 1, 5, and 7.

Good Match. Supportive, friendly, promising; 2, 3, and 11.

Ambitious Match. Full of potential but needs work; 4, 6, 8, 22, 33, and 44.

A Neutral Match. Could go either way, depends on maturity; 9

# 2

# Life Path 2: The Empathic Diplomat with a Black Belt in People-Pleasing

If a 1 is the steamroller boss who charges into life yelling "Follow me!," then 2 is the emotionally intelligent negotiator gently whispering, "Let's talk about our feelings first, mmkay?"

2s are the lovers, mediators, and peacemakers of the numerology world. They walk through life with their hearts wide open, their radar up, and a pocket full of tissues, just in case you start crying, and they will cry right alongside you.

These are the people who apologize when you bump into them. They are soft souls wrapped in silk, but don't mistake their sensitivity for weakness. They can detect a vibe shift from across the room, decode micro-expressions like a CIA profiler, and bring two enemies to a truce over tea and gluten-free cookies.

Let's unpack the beautiful, emotionally rich, slightly co-dependent magic of a 2.

2s don't just notice feelings, they absorb them. If you're sad, they're sad. If you're happy, they're still worried about that thing you were sad about the other day.

Empathy is their default setting. They pick up on tones, facial twitches, vague pauses in text messages, and your subtle change in punctuation. "Oh no," they'll say, "he ended that sentence with a period. He's definitely upset."

They're basically emotional seismographs: delicate, precise, and always registering something. 2s are highly intuitive, but they rarely brag about it. Instead, they just know things. Like how their friend is secretly mad, or that the waiter is going through a breakup, or that a storm is coming because their elbow hurts, and the energy feels "off."

They don't always know how they know; they just do. It's a gift, and sometimes a curse. Especially when they can sense you're lying about being "fine," and now they're worried, spiraling, and googling "how to help emotionally avoidant people."

2s are born mediators. They can sit between two raging people and somehow get them to calmly discuss their issues using "I" statements and deep breathing. If there's a disagreement, a 2 will not sleep until everyone feels heard and validated, even if they have to emotionally contort themselves into a pretzel to do it.

Spoiler: they're not. They're just constantly in repair mode.

**But also... They can't say no.**

If you've ever seen someone agree to something while clearly panicking on the inside, congratulations, you've spotted a stressed-out 2, who are notoriously bad at saying no. Why? Because they care. And also, because they worry that if they decline your offer to help move apartments during a heatwave, you'll never speak to them again. I'm not kidding...that's how their brains work.

They will say yes while dying inside. They will offer to help even when their to-do list is in flames. Then they'll cry in the shower and wonder why no one helps them the same way. Boundaries? They've heard of them. They've read books about them. They may even own a journal dedicated to them. But practicing them? Yeah, that's... complicated.

2s are the romantic idealists of the numerology world. They believe in soulmates, meaningful glances, and synchronizing Spotify playlists. When in love, they'll go above and beyond to nurture, support, and text you "just checking in" at precisely the moment you were about to fall apart.

They notice everything: your moods, your sighs, your sudden silence. They may not always ask directly what's wrong, but they know. And they're already planning how to fix it, quietly, lovingly, without making a scene.

Just be careful not to mistake their kindness for a lack of strength. 2s can, and will, walk away when they've had enough. It just might take three years of inner conflict, journaling, and asking their friends, "Do you think it's time?" before they do.

When overwhelmed, they may withdraw, cry in indirect metaphors, or express displeasure through overwatered plants and forced smiles. If you ask them what's wrong, they'll say, "Nothing, I'm fine," while emanating the energy of a tragic Victorian heroine. If they feel unappreciated, overextended, or like they've been giving from an empty cup for too long, their people-pleasing can morph into low-key resentment. And you will know, because they'll text you *"sure"* with a period.

Harmonizing any group of chaotic humans into something that feels oddly peaceful. Knowing when someone needs a hug before that person even knows it. The ability to forgive a lot, though they never forget, and they definitely have a file in their brain. Turning basic acts of kindness into deeply spiritual moments. Looking soft while actually being made of unyielding emotional steel.

## Spotting a 2 in the Wild:

Come Closer. I'm Safe. I Brought Snacks. If people had energy subtitles, a 2 would constantly be broadcasting:

"I'm not a threat. You can talk to me. I'll never judge your ugly cry."

Their body language is soft, open, and utterly inviting, like an unspoken group hug with excellent emotional boundaries (on a good day).

**Soft gestures.** No flailing, no finger-pointing, no dramatic air-chopping. A 2s gestures are like their favorite conflict resolution method: gentle, subtle, and soothing. Expect slow hand movements, thoughtful nods, and the occasional reassuring shoulder pat that says, "I feel you."

**Eye contact that comforts.** They look you in the eyes, not to intimidate, but to connect. It's sincere, steady, and often paired with a knowing tilt of the head like, "Tell me your truth, and I'll hold space for it."

**Open posture.** 2s don't cross their arms unless they're cold. Their body says, "You're welcome here." They angle toward you, lean in slightly, and subconsciously remove any emotional landmines before you even speak.

**Mirroring.** Without realizing it, they'll start to mimic your body language, because they're emotionally syncing with you like Bluetooth. If you shift, they shift. If you scratch your head, they do too. No, it's not creepy, it's empathic osmosis.

**Smiling... A lot.** 2s' smiles are like emotional Wi-Fi. They're always on. Whether they're happy, nervous, or gently defusing a tense moment, you'll see a soft, encouraging smile that says, "You're doing great, sweetie."

**Non-confrontational movements.** They don't invade your space. They don't loom. And they definitely don't do that thing where they slam their palms on the table mid-meeting. Their style is calm, grounded, and designed to soothe, not scare.

## The Dating Style of a 2:

Romantic, empathic, and possibly already planning your birthday six months in advance. If a 1 dates like a CEO scheduling meetings between power lunches, then Life Path 2 dates like someone who just knows your moon sign and brought tissues to your emotional breakdown.

They're not just looking for love.

They're looking for deep soul connection, emotional safety, shared playlists, and possibly handholding in the rain. 2s want the real thing. The "talk about our feelings for hours" thing. The "I noticed you were quieter today, so I brought your favorite cookies" kind of thing. They don't just date, they invest emotionally, intuitively, and with the emotional depth of an indie holiday film protagonist.

**Dating a 2 feels like:**

Being seen in a way that makes you slightly uncomfortable… but also deeply validated. Having your favorite comfort foods appear at just the right moment. Receiving texts that say, "Just thinking about you, no pressure, take your time replying. Feeling like you're being loved gently, even when you don't love yourself that day.

2s are drawn to partners who meet them in the emotional middle, people who can laugh freely, cry at Pixar movies, and then actually talk about why. They're looking for kindness and softness, not perfection, and they light up when someone notices their quiet efforts and says thank you (bonus points if it's often). Loyalty is everything to a 2, as is depth; they want someone who can dive into meaningful conversations without always rushing to fix things. For them, love feels best when it's mutual, steady, and built on the small, everyday gestures that say, "I see you."

They're not looking for chaos. So don't be that.

If you ghost a 2, it will spiritually wound them. And if you text "k" instead of "okay," they will read into it for three full days. Not kidding.

**The catch?** They sometimes disappear into their partner's needs.

2s are so focused on you that they sometimes forget that they exist. They'll say, "I'm fine" while making you dinner, folding your laundry, and quietly weeping inside because you forgot the anniversary of your first inside joke. They have the heart of a healer and the spine of a jellyfish when they're in love, until they hit their limit. And then? Silent treatment. (But, like, soft, silent treatment. With sad eyes.)

## Dating and Flirt Style of a 2: Masculine Edition

The 2 man is the understated romantic, the one who listens so closely, you forget you're on a date and start confessing your whole emotional autobiography. He doesn't rush the process. He builds trust gently, through meaningful conversations, small gestures, and that uncanny ability to remember everything you say. He's the guy who holds the door, offers his jacket, notices when you're overwhelmed, and then does something thoughtful without being asked. His flirting is subtle but sincere: think glances that linger, texts that check in, and questions that show he's not just interested in your story, but your soul. A 2 man leads with emotional intelligence, loyalty, and quiet devotion. If he chooses you, it's not a fling; it's because he sees long-term potential, and he's already imagining how to support your best self.

## Strengths in Love

**Unmatched emotional intuition.** They'll know something is wrong before you do and offer support before you can articulate it. They understand what you say, even though it comes out like a whining chihuahua.

**Loyalty to a fault.** They will love you through hard times, bad moods, and even your regrettable beard phase.

**Peacekeeping energy.** Fights with a 2 usually sound like, "I just want to understand how we both feel and move through this in a way that honors us." (Unless they've held in their frustration too long... Then it's tears, not tantrums. But if a 2 does go into a tantrum, then buddy, you done messed up big.)

**Romantic AF.** Poems. Handmade playlists. Eye contact like warm soup. Need I say more?

**Boundary who?** 2s may forget they have needs. Or they remember... and feel guilty for them.

**Over-accommodating.** They will change their schedule, haircut, and favorite meal to please a partner if they think it will help. (Note: It usually doesn't.)

**Avoiding conflict like it's the plague.** If there's tension, they might try to fix it with cookies. Not communication. Just cookies.

**Taking things very personally.** You said, "I don't care where we eat." They heard, "I'm emotionally unavailable and indifferent to your love."

A 2 needs a partner who appreciates the emotional labor they go through. Someone who checks in and says, "But how are you feeling?" A safe space where they can voice their real needs without worrying it'll cause a breakup. A gentle reminder that love doesn't mean disappearing into someone else.

**Dating advice for 2s (From someone who loves you):**

You don't need to earn love by over giving.

Saying no doesn't mean you're unkind.

Your needs are not inconveniences.

If someone loves you, they want to know what you want for dinner. (Seriously, just tell them.)

Dating a 2 is like dating the human version of a warm blanket that also wrote a heartfelt letter to your soul. They're sweet, loyal, emotionally tuned-in, and committed to harmony... almost to a fault. They don't just want love; they want meaningful, mutual, telepathic, "let's talk about our childhoods" kind of love. And if they find it, they'll give everything they have to make it work. Just remind them they don't have to give it all to be worthy of receiving love back.

**What to do when dating a 2**

(AKA: How to date a sweetheart without accidentally breaking them)

Dating a 2 is like holding a living, breathing Hallmark card that occasionally forgets to eat because they're busy worrying about your needs. They're romantic, gentle, and emotionally tuned-in, but if you mishandle that sensitivity? Prepare to be ghosted, and that never ends well.

Here's how to love one right (and avoid becoming the reason they write sad poetry under moonlight).

**DO:**

**Do say, "Thank you." Often.** They will absolutely over-deliver in the love department. Your job? Notice. Appreciate. Say "thank you" like it's your love language, even if they only brought you water. That water has intentions.

**Do reassure them regularly.** 2s can pick up on energetic static that hasn't even happened yet. They'll ask if you're mad because your tone changed slightly. Just reassure them. A lot. Say things like, "I love you," "You're doing great," and "No, I didn't mean that 'ok' text as a declaration of war."

**Do ask how they feel.** They're so used to caretaking that they forget they're allowed to be cared for. Asking, "What do you need?" may short-circuit them emotionally, but they'll adore you forever for it.

**Do take their advice seriously.** They've been quietly observing your patterns since date three. Their advice will be kind, useful, and eerily accurate. Listen to it. (And maybe apologize for not listening sooner.)

**Do hug them. Often.** Their love language is all the love languages. Physical affection? Yes. Words of affirmation? Absolutely. Holding their hand during a stressful moment? Marriage material.

## DON'T:

**Don't be vague.** "I'm just going through something" will be interpreted as "I don't love you anymore, and I'm planning my escape." Be honest, even if it's messy. 2s can handle the truth; they just can't handle the emotional guessing game.

**Don't take without giving.** A 2 will offer the moon. Don't just pocket it and ghost them emotionally. Give back. Show up. Meet them halfway. And don't assume their unconditional support comes with zero emotional cost.

**Don't mistake kindness for weakness.** They're gentle, not doormats. Push them far enough, and they will vanish like mist, armed with emotional intelligence and a perfectly written closure text you'll reread through tears for years.

**Don't use sarcasm as a shield.** Your "jokes" about commitment or emotions? Not cute to a 2. They'll smile politely, then spiral in silence for 48 hours, wondering if you were serious. Just say what you mean. Kindly.

**Don't dismiss their sensitivity.** Yes, they cried at that commercial. And yes, they noticed you didn't say goodnight with your usual emoji. Don't tell them they're "too sensitive." Their sensitivity is their superpower. Respect it or prepare for emotional eviction.

**Emergency affirmations (for the 2 and their partner):**

**For the 2:**

"I am allowed to have needs and express them without guilt."

"My love is a gift, not a transaction."

"Setting boundaries is healthy. Even if my voice shakes."

"I don't need to fix everything to be lovable."

**For their partner:**

"I will tell them I appreciate them even if they already know."

"I will not say 'I'm fine' when I'm clearly not."

"I will ask if they're okay when they suddenly start cleaning the kitchen while humming Adele.

"I will never, ever say 'You're too sensitive' unless I want to lose this soft-hearted angel forever."

Dating a 2 is a gift wrapped in empathy, tied with a bow of emotional nuance, and sprinkled with glittering loyalty. Treat them like the soulful treasure they are, and you'll have a partner who loves you with their whole heart, defends you with soft words, and remembers your childhood dog's name.

Screw it up, and you'll end up in one of their journals... filed under "Lessons I'll Never Repeat."

## Spiritual Lesson: You're Not a Doormat, Darling

2s are learning the art of boundaries, discernment, and valuing themselves as much as they value others. The universe didn't send them here to be everyone's emotional Sherpa. They're here to teach empathy with strength, and they're at their best when they stop over-accommodating and start honoring their own needs.

*Debra Zachau*

When a 2 steps into their power, they become unstoppable nurturers, conscious connectors, and intuitive guides. Their sensitivity becomes a gift to the world, not a burden on their backs.

Being around a 2 feels like sipping tea with someone who actually listens to you. They're calm in a crisis, supportive in a storm, and quietly wise in ways you didn't realize until after they've left, and suddenly everything makes sense.

They don't shout to be heard. They don't bulldoze to be respected. They bring gentleness, grace, and just enough emotional intelligence to quietly run the world, if only someone would ask them.

**From a Life Path 2s perfect partner perspective:**

Great Match. Easy flow, natural understanding; 2, 4, 8, 22, and 44.

Good Match. Supportive, friendly, promising; 1, 3, 6, 9, and 33.

Ambitious Match. Full of potential but needs work; 5, 7, and 11.

# 3

# Life Path 3: The Sparkling Communicator Who Might Crack a Joke Mid-Sentence... and Still be Charming

3s are the joyful glitter of the numerology world. These are the people who talk with their hands, laugh at their own jokes, and somehow turn a trip to the grocery store into an improvised stand-up set. Creative, expressive, and emotionally vibrant, 3s are wired to make the world more beautiful, heartfelt, and dramatic.

If 1s walk in with a mission and 2s walk in with a hug, 3s enter the room mid-story, with twinkle lights, snacks, and several half-finished art projects they can't wait to show you.

But don't be fooled by the sparkle. Underneath their upbeat vibe is a deeply emotional being who feels everything deeply and often out loud.

There's something unmistakable about a 3. They radiate a kind of creative intensity that feels like standing near a glitter cannon; you never quite know what's about to happen, but you're pretty sure it'll be interesting. At their best, 3s are emotional alchemists, taking their inner world and turning it into poetry, performance, or at least a killer Instagram caption.

Their creativity isn't a quiet whisper; it's a full-blown parade. 3s are the artistic souls of numerology, and their minds never stop generating ideas. Whether it's painting, writing, music, acting, or interpretive sock-puppet theater (yes, really), they need a way to get the storm of feelings and visions out of their heads and into the world. And when they do? Magic.

Their humor is magnetic. A 3 can find the funny in almost any situation, often turning personal pain into public comedy with surprising depth. It's not that they don't feel things; it's that they feel everything and instinctively know how to package it for the collective good. It's part self-defense, part art form, and completely effective.

When it comes to charm, 3s don't work at it; they just are. Their presence is warm, witty, and captivating. People gravitate toward them because their natural storytelling and openness create an atmosphere of instant connection. They're the kind of person who makes you feel like you're the only one in the room, right up until they start a conga line.

Words are their playground. 3s are communicators to their core. They know how to get a message across, whether spoken, written, sung, or posted in all caps with emojis. Many 3s become writers, influencers, podcasters, or performers, not just because they can, but because they have to. It's how they breathe.

And even when life falls apart (which it will, because 3s live dramatically), they bounce back with the emotional resilience of a rom-com heroine after a makeover montage. They'll call it a "plot twist," make you laugh about it, and probably write a song before the dust settles. Their optimism isn't naïve; it's survival.

Socially, 3s are naturals. Put one in a room full of strangers and check back in twenty minutes; they'll be leading karaoke, giving impromptu speeches, and referring to at least three people as their new best friends.

Now, let's talk about the flip side. Every dazzling disco ball has its dark side, and 3 is no exception. For all their shine, 3s can unravel spectacularly when they're feeling insecure, overwhelmed, or, heaven forbid, ignored.

When they're not getting the attention or affirmation they thrive on, 3s might turn up the volume instead of pausing for reflection. Suddenly, a charming anecdote becomes an exaggerated sob story, a TikTok becomes a cry for help with filters, and their signature "I'm fine!" starts sounding suspiciously like emotional deflection.

One of the biggest traps for a 3 is superficiality. In an effort to keep everything light, breezy, and non-threatening, they may start skimming the surface of life. Serious conversations? Too heavy. Difficult emotions? Better make a joke. If things get uncomfortable, they might ghost reality and escape into distractions, entertainment, or a new creative project they'll abandon by Thursday.

That endless stream of creative ideas can also lead to chaos. With so many possibilities, how can they choose just one? They start seventeen things, finish maybe two, and spend the rest of the time convincing themselves it was all part of their artistic process.

Behind their dazzling smile, many 3s carry a quiet insecurity. They might mask it with charisma, storytelling, or a well-timed self-deprecating joke, but deep down, they crave validation and often fear they're not enough unless they're performing.

Impulsiveness is another shadow trait. Fueled by inspiration and passion, they can make dramatic decisions that feel like genius in the moment but look like chaos in hindsight. "Let's move to Italy and open a bookstore-wine bar-bakery with goats!" Sounds magical until the lease is signed and the goats arrive.

When hurt, 3s might lash out with passive-aggressive sarcasm or vanish altogether, leaving behind an emotional cliffhanger worthy of its own Netflix special. Their sensitivity is real, but it doesn't always come out in the healthiest ways.

The final trap? Avoidance. 3s don't always face pain; they dance around it. They change the subject. They make it rhyme. They create art about it instead of sitting with it. But true healing for a 3 comes when they realize they don't have to entertain to be loved, they just have to be real.

3s remind us that joy is sacred, and creativity is a life force. They show us how to turn vulnerability into art, how to laugh in the middle of heartbreak, and how to speak truth in a way that sticks.

They are born to uplift, connect, and remind us that it's okay to feel everything out loud.

At their highest expression, 3s are artistic healers. At their lowest? Beautiful disasters with a great soundtrack. Either way, we're watching. And we're laughing. And we love them for it.

## How to Spot a 3 in the Wild

3s have a presence you feel. They're creative professionals, charismatic problem-solvers, and living proof that being expressive and being effective aren't mutually exclusive.

**The laughter.** It's frequent, contagious, and yes, they do laugh at their own jokes. Not because they're trying to steal the spotlight, but because joy is the call for their people.

**The quotes**. Their devices, journals, mugs, and possibly forearms are decorated with affirmations. Some are borrowed from legends; others are 100% original. (One was a typo that became a mantra.)

**Their conversations.** Equal parts strategy session, creative brainstorm, and unexpected group therapy. There may be charts, jokes, and at least one surprising mic-drop insight that leaves you stunned and oddly inspired.

To the untrained eye, it might look like a colorful cyclone of ideas. But to a 3? It's not chaos, it's clarity with personality.

## The Dating Style of a 3

A 3 doesn't enter a date; they arrive. Possibly with jazz hands. Definitely with a story. Their energy is so vivid that it might feel like you're suddenly on a talk show. They sparkle, they joke, they complement the waiter's accent and invent a backstory for it. Within minutes, you'll either be intrigued or totally overwhelmed. Sometimes both.

What they lack in chill, they make up for in charm. You won't leave the first date wondering what they thought of you; they'll have sorted that out halfway through dessert. You'll laugh more than you expected. You'll feel seen. You'll feel special. You'll feel like maybe you should've worn nicer shoes.

3s don't date you. They romance you like it's a theatrical production with a surprise finale and themed merchandise. Expect personalized playlists, spontaneous love notes, and dates that involve food trucks, stargazing, or impromptu salsa lessons in the living room. They'll make you laugh. They'll flirt like it's a sport. And they'll probably tell you all about their childhood trauma in a wildly charming monologue that makes you laugh and tear up.

They express love the same way they express everything else: loudly, often, and usually with flair. They'll send memes, playlists, voice notes, and possibly an interpretive sketch of what your relationship could be in five years (if Mercury stays out of retrograde).

Do they fall fast? Sometimes. But it's not always about forever, it's about the feeling in the moment. When they're in love, they're in deep... until the feeling changes. Which it might. Often. Because 3s are ruled by inspiration, not norms.

Here's the thing: 3s are lovers of potential. And that means sometimes they're more in love with the idea of you than the actual you. They can get swept up in fantasy, only to crash land in reality and wonder why it's not quite as magical when you're folding laundry instead of doing karaoke.

They want to feel inspired, not boxed in. When things get serious, they may disappear into a flurry of new projects, new people, or that ex who still likes their stories on Instagram. It's not that they don't care, it's that they're easily distracted by shiny things, and emotional fireworks.

They also fear monotony as if it were a contagious disease. If your idea of a perfect relationship is weekly tacos and reruns of your favorite sitcom, a 3 may start scanning the horizon for more variety. If you're aware of this in advance and still want weekly tacos and reruns, then you won't be surprised at the upcoming crankiness from your 3.

Dating a 3 is fun. It's noisy. It's spontaneous. It's Instagram-able. But it also requires patience. They feel deeply and express loudly. They're not trying to be dramatic; their internal world is dramatic. And because they love through performance and creativity, they often need constant feedback to feel secure.

And then there's the attention issue. If you seem distracted or uninterested, they might spiral. They don't just notice emotional distance; they feel it. And they will absolutely try to fix it with a grand gesture, a dramatic exit, or 23 texts with escalating emoji usage.

They may not always say what they mean. They may joke instead of opening up. But when they trust you enough to show you their real feelings underneath the performance, that's when the relationship deepens into something truly special, even permanent.

## Dating Style of a 3: Masculine Edition

A 3 man is pure charm in motion. He flirts like he was born doing it, and honestly, he probably was. Conversation? Effortless. Humor? On point. His gift is connection, and he knows how to make you feel like the most fascinating person in the room (even if he's lowkey stealing the spotlight). But don't mistake his playfulness for lack of depth, when a 3 man is serious about you, he'll open up his creative world and invite you in. He's expressive, emotionally intuitive, and surprisingly thoughtful, often showing love through spontaneous gestures, inside jokes, and the kind of compliments that feel specific, not scripted. His ideal date? Something fun, flirty, and just a little unconventional, because if it feels like a scene from a rom com, he's in his element. His dating style is a mix of laughter, honesty, and colorful storytelling, with a dash of "did he just write me a poem?"

**When dating a 3**

**DO:**

**Do praise their creativity.** They need it like plants need water. And they'll bloom every time.

**Do laugh with them.** Humor is their first language.

**Do encourage their dreams**, even the weird ones. "Yes, start that pet tarot reading business!"

**Do match their energy when possible.** Or at least admire it from a safe distance.

**Do let them be the center of attention sometimes**. They don't need the spotlight constantly, but they need to know it's there.

**DON'T:**

**Don't ghost them.** Radio silence feels like emotional exile.

**Don't mock their enthusiasm.** They know they're extra. They're proud of it.

**Don't shut down emotional conversations**. If you go quiet, they go existential.

**Don't dismiss their creative projects**, even if they abandon half of them. The process is the point.

**Don't force them into a box**. Relaxed routine is okay. Rigid schedules? Soul death.

**Don't stifle them**. They'll either rebel... or start writing cryptic poetry about you on social media.

**Emergency Affirmations for Dating a 3:**

When you find yourself overwhelmed by the energy, passion, or six back-to-back ideas for a "shared creative business," try one of these:

"This is not chaos. This is color."

"They are not trying to exhaust me on purpose."

"If I give it thirty minutes, they'll circle back to calm."

"This story probably has a point."

"Yes, they wrote me a poem instead of texting back. That is love, in their language."

They will romance you like a sunrise in Paris, dazzling, dramatic, and maybe a bit much for a Thursday. But if you can ride the waves of their energy, respect their need for expression, and not panic when they start crying during a commercial... you'll experience a relationship full of joy, depth, and fun artistic chaos. In love, they want to be seen, celebrated, and free to be their whole, brilliant selves. If you can offer that, a 3 will light up your life in ways you never imagined and probably write about it later.

## Life Path 3 Spiritual Lessons

The soul of a 3 came here to rediscover the sacred power of self-expression. Their spiritual lesson? To speak, write, sing, dance, create, giggle, emote, and actually mean it. They're here to learn that their words hold weight, and that avoiding emotional truth in favor of being "likable" or entertaining is a spiritual cul-de-sac. 3s often spend years second-guessing their value, only to learn (sometimes the hard way) that vulnerability is their actual superpower. When they embrace their feelings instead of airbrushing them, their message becomes magnetic.

And what do they teach the rest of us?

That life is a canvas, not a checklist. That joy isn't trivial; it's healing. And that laughter, when used with heart, can be a divine force that brings people together and gives pain a place to exhale. 3s remind us that beauty belongs in the everyday, and that telling your story might just save someone else's.

When focused, they are wildly productive creatives who can bring big ideas to life; projects, books, courses, businesses, you name it. They may seem whimsical, but under all that sparkle is a mind that's sharp, emotionally tuned-in, and surprisingly strategic. They lead with light, and they're rooted in substance.

**From a Life Path 3's perspective. Their perfect partner:**

Great Match. Easy flow, natural understanding; 3, and 5.

Good Match. Supportive, friendly, promising; 1, 2, and 11.

Ambitious Match. Full of potential but needs work; 4, 7, 8, 22, and 44.

A Neutral Match. Could go either way, depends on maturity; 6, 9, and 33.

# 4

# Life Path 4: The Organizational Whisperer (and Closet Romantic)

If 3 is the party planner, a 4 is the person who shows up early to set up folding chairs, tables, and place cards... perfectly, thank you very much.

These are the structure-lovers, the calendar-color-coders, the ones who actually read the instruction manual and take quiet offense when you don't. 4s are the backbone of every functioning society, business, and extended family potluck. Without them, buildings wouldn't stay up, laws wouldn't get enforced, and nobody would ever change the printer ink.

But before you assume they're all pocket protectors and orthopedic shoes, let's be clear: 4s may not flaunt their flair, but they've got it, it's just laminated and filed under "Surprises." They are the sacred keepers of structure and logic, and the backbone of civilization.

If you've ever walked into someone's house and felt a strong desire to apologize for tracking in imaginary dirt... you've probably entered the home of a 4. These folks are the ones quietly (and sometimes not-so-quietly) holding society together with spreadsheets, dental floss, and a deep, abiding respect for any and all instruction manuals, tutorials, and community sign-up sheets.

**4s are the ones you can count on - always.**

They'll help you move, build your IKEA furniture correctly, and show up on time with snacks, receipts, and oh, backup snacks (just in case). They are painfully dependable. As in: if a 4 says they'll be somewhere at a specific time, you can start boiling the pasta.

But don't mistake their love of rules and systems for boring. 4s are secretly fascinating, once you get past their slightly intimidating exterior. Underneath the "I've got this" vibe is someone who genuinely has it but also wishes other people would at least try to meet them halfway. Or stop sabotaging them.

Their relationships are carefully curated. They're not interested in drama, chaos, or anything that involves vague expectations and unpaid invoices. A 4 likes loyalty, follow-through, and emotional predictability. They aren't into games, unless it's chess, and even then it better be regulation.

Their favorite phrase might as well be: "Let's be practical." Which, when translated, means "Let's make a plan and actually stick to it." A 4 is the kind of person who reads warranties and actually understands them. They are genuinely puzzled when you choose not to read your car manual cover to cover.

In love, friendship, or business partnerships, 4s bring loyalty, depth, and a powerful work ethic. They are builders of homes, of legacies, of relationships that don't collapse during the first disagreement. They may not be the type to sweep you off your feet with candlelit poetry (unless they're also a 3 on the cusp), but they'll show their love by assembling your furniture correctly and without visible screws.

They need security, emotional, and financial. They are attracted to stability, honesty, and people who follow through on what they say. If you flake on them more than twice, congratulations, you've been quietly demoted to "acquaintance."

In friendships, they're the ones you call when your car breaks down, your dog runs away, or your taxes confuse you. They'll show up with jumper cables, a leash, and a well-tabbed IRS guidebook. But don't forget to say thank you, they notice.

**The 4 in shadow.** Anxiety over accountability.

"Did I forget something?"

"Am I doing enough?"

"Is everyone relying on me? Should I be relying on me more?"

They don't freak out because they're lazy. They freak out because they care so deeply about being reliable that the possibility of failure haunts them like a poorly formatted flow chart presentation.

**Hyper-Criticism (With a Bunch of Self-Loathing!).**

Stress flips the inner perfectionist switch to max volume. Suddenly, nothing is good enough, not the work, not the coworkers, not themselves. They'll find fault in everything, including how their toast came out this morning. And you can be sure they'll let you know, "This isn't toasted. It's moist bread with grill marks." They may also get judgy toward others, not because they're mean, but because "If I have to be perfect, why are you allowed to wing it?"

Stress doesn't always make a 4 speed up; it can make them freeze. Like a deer in headlights, except the deer has three overdue reports, a half-cooked dinner, and a self-help podcast playing in the background. They may stare at their to-do list for hours, paralyzed by the fear that any choice might be the wrong one. Then they Google "how to make the perfect decision" until their phone dies.

The body keeps the score, and for 4s, that score is written in tension headaches, back pain, clenching jaws, and unexplained gut issues. You'll know they're stressed when they walk like their spine has filed a formal complaint or they're reaching for the ibuprofen like they're breath mints.

When overwhelmed, they often retreat. They'll go full hermit mode, convinced that no one will understand and it's best to just "work it out" in silence. They might cancel plans, stop replying to texts, and disappear into a home-improvement project that nobody asked for. If a 4 is sanding cabinet doors at midnight, you should probably check in.

## How to Spot a 4 in the Wild

They're not the loudest one in the room, but they are the most grounded. While others are scanning the menu or the crowd, a 4 is already scanning for exits, clean bathrooms, and chairs that won't wobble. Their posture is usually upright, their handshake firm, and their clothing? Neat, well-fitted, and unlikely to include anything that says, "dry clean only."

You'll notice they tend to sit with intention, shoulders squared, feet planted, like they're prepared for both deep conversation and an earthquake. There's a calm, measured energy about them. They don't fidget much. Their phone is face-down or tucked away completely. If they're out with you, they're present, mentally and physically.

They observe before jumping in. They don't interrupt. They may raise one brow when someone exaggerates. They're the ones making mental notes rather than broadcasting opinions. And if you look closely, you might catch them subtly straightening the saltshaker or aligning their silverware. Not for show. Just... because it wasn't right.

They usually have a signature look, classic, consistent, and practical. Think: dark jeans, quality shoes, tidy hair, and a jacket that has exactly the right number of pockets. Their accessories are functional. Their vibe? Prepared but not flashy. They'll carry themselves like someone who knows where their car is parked and has definitely locked it twice.

So, if you're across the room wondering which one might help you build furniture without arguing or read the lease before you sign it, follow the trail of practical footwear, good posture, and quiet competence. That's your 4.

## The Dating Style of a 4

They are not going to sweep you off your feet with spontaneous rose petals or rooftop serenades. No, they'll carefully lay a foundation, make sure the weather's safe, and *then* invite you to stand on a very structurally sound porch for a well-timed hug. And honestly? That hug will probably mean more than a dozen whirlwind dates, because when a 4 opens their heart, it's not casual. It's for keeps. They're building a house from scratch. You won't be living in it by the second date, but when it's finally move-in ready? That thing will be solid, warm, and designed to survive emotional hurricanes. They don't lead with flash. They lead with function. You might not notice them at first in the room, but give it five minutes, and you'll be asking them how they manage to stay so organized, while secretly hoping they'll read over your rental lease.

They usually come across as calm, competent, and slightly reserved. But don't forget that spontaneous dry humor that can sneak into the party and surprise you. There's a quiet confidence about them that says, "I pay my bills early," and frankly, that's hot. They may not flirt with grand gestures, but they will remember your coffee order and your dog's name, which, in my opinion…, is even hotter.

They don't do "game playing." If they like you, you'll know because they'll tell you in a sentence that's been carefully considered for 48 hours and delivered with appropriate punctuation.

They date like they build, with patience, intention, and a backup plan. You won't be whisked off to Paris on a whim, but you will be invited on a well-researched hike, with water bottles, sunscreen, and a rain poncho (just in case). They don't want to fall in love; they want to grow into it. Like a tomato plant. A very emotionally stable tomato plant.

They're excellent listeners, even if they don't always offer flowery replies. Instead of poetry, they show up on time. Instead of love songs, they fix the broken cabinet in your kitchen. You'll start to notice: their affection isn't loud, but it's consistent. And consistency, in dating, is a wildly underrated kink.

## Dating and Flirt Style of a 4: Masculine Edition

A 4 man dates like he builds everything else: with intention, structure, and a quiet sense of responsibility. He's not flashy or mysterious; he's dependable. If he says he'll pick you up at 7, you'd better be ready at 6:57. He shows affection through actions, not declarations. He'll fix your sink before he writes you a love poem, but hey, your sink won't leak anymore. His idea of romance isn't about grand gestures; it's about follow-through. He listens carefully, remembers the details, and slowly builds trust like it's a brick house meant to last.

Dating him feels steady, safe, even. He might not always say what he feels in the moment, but if he's there, investing his time and energy, he's serious. He doesn't waste effort on maybe. A 4 man loves by showing up, showing care, and showing you that he's not going anywhere. That's his version of fireworks, consistency, loyalty, and a deep sense of "I got you."

Dating a 4, man or woman, means dating someone who sees patterns and has opinions about them. That includes how you butter toast, how you organize your kitchen drawers, and whether you should be wearing socks on hardwood floors. (Safety first).

They don't always realize that their "helpful suggestions" feel like criticism. But rest assured, it's not that they think you're doing life wrong; they just think there's a better way. And that way involves containers. And labels.

Flexibility can be a struggle. 4s are comforted by predictability, and spontaneous changes of plan may cause an emotional "404 Error." Try moving a weekend getaway to a surprise location and watch their soul briefly leave their body.

They can also take their sweet time in deciding if someone is "worth the investment." If you're in a hurry to fall in love, you'll have better luck with a 2 or 6 person. But if you're looking for someone who means what they say and plans for the long haul, you're in the right place.

**DO**:

**Do appreciate their loyalty.** Once a 4 is in, they're in. No games. No backdoors. Just full-hearted loyalty and a drawer they cleared out for your stuff.

**Do respect their routines.** Changing plans at the last minute is like throwing glitter at a librarian; just don't.

**Do be patient with their pace.** They're building a stable future, not a rom-com montage. Let them set the tempo.

**Do recognize their love language.** Acts of service, baby. If they fixed your tire, made you dinner, and scheduled your dentist appointment, they love you.

**Do show up when you say you will.** Flakiness is the ultimate betrayal. They won't yell, but they will never forget.

**DON'T:**

**Don't try to rush their feelings.** They won't fall in love on cue. And if you push too hard, they'll dig in harder.

**Don't mock their need for structure.** That weekly meal plan isn't boring. It's sacred.

**Don't dismiss their concerns as "overthinking".** They've already thought of 12 possible outcomes, and only half involve emotional ruin.

**Don't be inconsistent.** If your affection fluctuates, they'll assume you're not reliable. (And 4s only build with reliable materials.)

**Don't interrupt their sacred alone time.** They need silence to recharge. Don't take it personally if they don't want to talk.

**Affirmations when Dating a 4**

"Just because they don't say it every day doesn't mean they don't love me."

"Spreadsheets are romantic in their own way."

"They're not avoiding my emotions, they're categorizing them."

"This is the most faithful, responsible love I've ever had... and that's kind of sexy."

"I am not a mess. I am an invitation to spontaneity. It's fine."

## Spiritual Lessons: The sacred order of things.

Spiritually, 4s are learning that structure isn't just physical, it's metaphysical. Their souls are here to master the balance between control and trust, logic and faith.

Their challenge? Loosening the grip. Letting go of the need to manage every outcome, to ensure every duck is in a row (and wearing matching outfits). They often struggle to believe that things can work out without their constant vigilance.

The spiritual lesson for a 4 is that inner order matters just as much as outer order. That it's okay if some things don't make sense right away. That life can be beautiful, even when it's messy. That sometimes the best plan... is no plan. (Oops, cue panic.)

They also need to learn to receive help. They will drag a broken couch up three flights of stairs alone before asking for assistance. Why? Because asking means vulnerability and ensuring reciprocity is immediate. But vulnerability is strength, and that's the big soul lesson.

When they soften, when they trust the process, when they believe the universe can handle some of the heavy lifting? That's when the magic starts.

At their highest potential, they're the architects of stability. They build the frameworks that others dance upon. They make dreams happen with planning, patience, and a decent stapler. And while they might not always be the loudest in the room, they're often the reason the room hasn't collapsed.

**From a Life Path 4's perspective. Their perfect partner:**

Great Match. Easy flow, natural understanding; 2, 4, 8, 22, and 44.

Good Match. Supportive, friendly, promising; 6, 7, and 33.

Ambitious Match. Full of potential but needs work; 1, 3, 5, and 11.

# 5

# Life Path 5: The Freedom-Loving Wild Card Who Makes Life Feel Like a Road Trip... with No GPS

If you've ever tried to pin down a 5, you already know it's like hugging a hummingbird: thrilling, beautiful, and slightly exhausting. The most fidgety Life Path inside the numerology network. People born a 5 are natural adventurers, charmers, and more comfortable with change than the rest of us. Their soul contract might as well say: "I solemnly swear to never do the same thing twice, unless it was thrilling the first time." They are passionate until distracted. Dedicated... until another adventure calls. They are unforgettable. When a 5 walks into your life, the air changes. You laugh harder, dream bigger, and for a while at least, you truly believe in magic.

A 5 has a passport full of stamps (or at least 14 open tabs for flight deals). Their minds are wired for movement, mental, physical, and spiritual. "Settling down" sounds suspiciously like "giving up." They live for the plot twist, the pivot, the pop-up art gallery that only exists for one night in a warehouse with no signage. These are the people who reinvent themselves every few years, not because they're lost, but because they found something better. A new hobby. A better major to study. A more flexible job. One that lets them work in Bali. Or their car.

Their love for adventure and change might lead them to try new things, meet new people, or explore the many different groups at the party. When relaxed, they either share their adventures and travels with others or sit mesmerized, listening to the stories of freedom told by others. They will gravitate to those who may match their desire for freedom and plan a trip or project around the topic. They will be comfortable with or without a partner if unattached; however, if married, they will conscientiously include their spouse in all conversations.

They are entrepreneurial and persuasive. Seriously, you will find yourself buying whatever they're selling, whether it's a startup idea or a last-minute road trip. But here's the flip side: routine is their nemesis. Monotony is their slow death. You ask a 5 to commit to a five-year plan, and their spirit will astral project out of the room before you finish the sentence. They need options, especially within the boundaries of a commitment.

Romantic relationships with a 5 are like dating fireworks. Dazzling. Electric. Occasionally illegal in some states. They crave connection, excitement, and someone who understands that commitment doesn't mean confinement. A partner who can love them without trying to own them will win their heart. They will fall in love with you so deeply that, on the days you wish they'd leave, they won't. But the flip side: clinginess from a partner gives them hives. So does routine. Now you know how you can get them out of the house. Show them a list of chores with a deadline. Ba-bye. (Ah, alone at last.)

They're not emotionally shallow, quite the opposite. However, they express love in bursts of spontaneity rather than idealistic visions. You won't get a five-year anniversary scrapbook. You might get surprise concert tickets and a kiss in the rain.

Friendships with 5s are exhilarating but sometimes inconsistent. They'll disappear for six months, then text you from Machu Picchu like nothing happened. "Miss you! Let's do karaoke next week." And the worst part? You'll excitedly say yes.

Despite their reputation for flakiness (which, let's be honest, can sometimes be well-earned), they possess a focused momentum that, when lit by inspiration, becomes downright unstoppable. These are not just adrenaline junkies hopping from thrill to thrill, they're intuitive truth-seekers with the uncanny ability to sniff out a story before it breaks. Many 5s are drawn to fields like journalism, broadcasting, or commentary, not because they crave the spotlight (okay, sometimes they do), but because they're wired to know and tell. Their communication skills are top-tier, often paired with a dazzling curiosity that makes them superb investigative journalists, cultural critics, or content creators. Whether it's exposing corruption or decoding pop culture in a viral YouTube rant, 5s have a talent for turning information into impact. Their creativity isn't just for show; it's got an edge. Where a 3 may invent an imaginary world, a 5 will hold a microphone, ask uncomfortable questions, and livestream the whole thing.

To unlock their full potential, a 5 must learn the art of building focus. This is the game-changer. If you're dating, working with, or related to a 5, you've probably already seen it: their brilliance can either explode into a sky full of fireworks or fizzle out the moment something gets hard or boring. A 5 with curiosity, creativity, and spontaneity *but no focus* is like trying to bottle a lightning storm with a spaghetti strainer. They become a beautiful handful, equal parts inspiring and exhausting. But when they learn to direct that energy? Stand back. You're about to witness lift-off. They inspire the rest of us to live a little louder, laugh a little harder, and try something new, even if it completely freaks us out, and somehow, we're always better for it.

Let's be honest, they aren't here for the easy stuff. They're here to live. But, that appetite for stimulation can come with side effects, such as restlessness. If they're not moving, they're thinking about moving. If they're not thinking about moving, they're probably distracting themselves with snacks, Instagram, or a new tattoo. Big choices are often made mid-conversation, fueled by inspiration or frustration. "I quit my job" and "I booked a camel trek" are uttered with the same casual vibe.

Calendars? What are those? They are organized emotionally but not always logistically. Their inbox is a war zone. Sometimes their quest for freedom sounds suspiciously like "I'm doing what I want, deal with it." Not great for roommates, co-workers, or spouses. They truly love the idea of showing up, and at the time of saying yes to getting together, they really intend to follow through... but reality may vary.

They hate to limit their options. Choosing a path feels like rejecting a hundred others, so they hover in the space between choices for longer than necessary. Their "YOLO" instincts can override common sense. (Helicopter ziplining at sunset? Sounds amazing. What could go wrong?) They want things now. Not soon. Now. And don't explain why it'll take time, and "don't just sit there," help them find a workaround.

## How to Spot a 5 in the Wild:

**Big, Expressive Gestures.** A 5 could read the weather report and present it in poetry slam fashion. Their hands draw pictures in the air. They can't help it; it's how they think out loud. Watch closely and you'll notice their gestures increase when they're excited or trying to convince you of something (which is always).

**Restless Movements.** You might think they're nervous, but really, their body's just playing jazz. They bounce on the balls of their feet. Their hands move even when their mouth isn't. If their legs aren't crossed, their foot is tapping. They're not anxious, they're alive.

**Open, Forward-Leaning Posture.** Whether sitting across from you or leaning across the table to share a half-formed idea, 5s lean in; literally. It's how they connect, how they show they're invested. There's no aloofness in a 5's physical presence. If they're with you, they're with you.

**Quick Reactions.** Their body will respond to your comment before their brain decides if it agrees. A raised eyebrow, a sudden laugh, a shift in their chair, they're reactive, and you can read them like a short story collection with a lot of plot twists. What's nice about this is that while doing your presentation, you'll be able to shift your words and cadence to suit the moment and elicit a positive outcome for yourself. When in doubt, rely on your 5 audience members to know when to shift the vibe while speaking.

**Unpolished but Charming.** You'll see the shirt untucked or the bag half-zipped. A wrinkle in their jacket. Nothing sloppy, just that "creative chaos" aesthetic. Life's too short to iron. They show up real, not rehearsed.

They're the ones talking with both their hands and eyebrows. They're wearing something slightly unconventional, but somehow, they pull it off. They're asking questions, interrupting themselves with ideas, and offering to start a group project no one asked for. They're already ten steps ahead in their mind and three tabs open on their browser.

A 5 in the wild is never just doing one thing. They're working, texting, voice-memoing a podcast idea, and also ordering sushi for lunch. They're magnetic, a little chaotic, and oddly trustworthy, because they're unapologetically themselves. They inspire, disrupt, create, and charm their way into progress. While traditional structures make them itchy, they know how to lead through excitement and connection.

## The Dating Style of a 5

If dating were a road trip, 5s would throw out the map, crank the music, and pick up three hitchhikers just to hear their stories. Romance for the 5 is about freedom, spontaneity, and the thrill of discovery. If you're looking for someone to sit beside you on the porch every night at 6 PM sharp, you might want to keep swiping.

They are charming, magnetic, and hard to miss. They come in like a sparkler, bright, bold, and just unpredictable enough to make your heart race. They'll have you laughing within the first five minutes and daydreaming about a weekend getaway by dessert. They're flirtatious, yes, but it's not fake. They genuinely love connecting with people; they just do it often.

Think of it less like a courtship and more like a guided jungle tour, one with unexpected detours, late-night texts, and spontaneous weekend adventures. A 5 might serenade you one night, disappear for two days, then reappear with plane tickets and a grin. They aren't playing games (usually), they're just wired for motion.

## Dating Style of a 5: Masculine Edition

Dating a 5 man is like grabbing a drink with Indiana Jones; he's charismatic, unpredictable, and always planning a spontaneous trip to somewhere you've never heard of. He flirts with wit, moves fast, and keeps things exciting. But here's the part most people miss when a 5 man chooses you, he's not just choosing love, he's choosing *home*. And that means something sacred.

As you have already found out he's not built for routine, but he is built for trust.

Once he's all in, he will look to his partner to help anchor him in a world he constantly wants to outrun. Not to control him, but to gently remind him that adventure doesn't have to mean escape. That structure doesn't kill freedom; it protects it. And if you've studied the numbers, you'll know when a 5 man marries, he's choosing someone who understands his restlessness without taking it personally.

He'll still dream aloud about you both becoming expats in Portugal or opening a beach bar in Bali, but deep down, he's counting on you to help filter the fantasy into something real. He doesn't want to be tied down; he wants to be held steady. There's a difference.

So, if you're dating a 5 man, expect passion, stories, and impulsive brilliance. But also know that when he calls you his person, he's asking you to be his anchor when the wind picks up. And that devotion? It runs deeper than he knows how to say, because when a 5 stays, it's not by accident. It's because he's finally found a partner in freedom.

**The shadow of 5:**

Let's be honest, dating a 5 is not for the faint of heart or the overly clingy. If you are a 2, 4, or 8 Life Path, run while your heart is still your own! Commitment can feel like confinement if they don't trust you with their need for space. They're allergic to micromanagement, reluctant to expectations, and will exit stage left if they feel cornered. If you guilt-trip a 5, you won't see them again, unless it's on your mutual friend's Instagram story in another country.

All is not lost even if they wander off for a bit.

Here's the truth. I've tested every number, and despite how this particular Life Path can seem about commitment, they become the exact opposite when they find someone who truly understands their quirks. The key? Noticing the signs of their restlessness before it spirals into a full-blown meltdown. Trust me, you'll feel the disruption in the force long before *they* admit something's off. If your 5 partner's been edgy or erratic for more than a couple of weeks, there's a pressure cooker building. It's not personal, it's existential. And when that pressure hits the boiling point, a 5 might quit a job, bail on a long-term commitment, or move to another city without so much as a group text.

Want to prevent chaos? Budget for it. No, seriously. Tuck away a "Save the 5" fund. Even if money's tight, stash a little for when their inner free spirit slams into the wall of routine. That pile of cash could become an impromptu weekend away, a new gadget, a kayak rental, or a deluxe drone with a camera that makes them feel alive again. Spontaneous indulgence is not irresponsible for a 5; it's maintenance.

Whatever you do, don't try to soothe them with lectures about long-term vision. Telling a 5 to "just be patient" is like asking a hummingbird to nap. Delayed gratification is not their love language. And asking them to "look forward" to something scheduled next month will only highlight how bored they are right now.

If your 5 keeps hitting this wall, same frustration, different month, it's time for a real, heart-to-heart reset. Ask: Do they need a new career? A high-stakes hobby that comes with a learning curve? A side hustle that lets them experiment and explore? Don't wait for the meltdown, talk it out before the volcano blows. You'll *both* thank yourselves later.

**If You've Found a 5, and Can't Stop Yourself from Falling in Love:**

**DO:**

**Do be spontaneous**. If you can improvise a date based on a wrong turn, you're winning.

**Do encourage their ideas.** And celebrate their latest obsessions, even if they change weekly.

**Do respect their independence**. They're not disappearing from you; they're disappearing into something interesting. Thinking you should be the only interesting thing in their life will develop an unfortunate perspective that will constantly leave you sad and bewildered. Remember, it's not personal.

**Do keep things fun**. If you're not laughing or learning, you're losing them. They're looking for a partner who's lit up by life, not just sitting back watching it go by.

**DON'T:**

**Don't demand a five-year plan**. You'll get a five-minute pause, tops.

**Don't get possessive**. They will Houdini out of clinginess with astonishing speed.

**Don't mistake their curiosity for disloyalty**. Just because they flirt doesn't mean they're cheating. It means they breathe.

**Don't interrupt them mid-anecdote**, especially when they're on a roll. A 5 in storytelling mode is not to be silenced.

**Emergency Affirmations if Dating a 5**

"They're not ghosting me; they're probably deep in a documentary rabbit hole about the Mariana Trench."

"This rollercoaster is thrilling because I bought a ticket, not because I'm trapped on it."

"I give them space, and they come back... eventually... with souvenirs, and maybe ice cream."

"Just because they forgot dinner plans doesn't mean they don't care. It means they got excited about something shiny."

"I can't change them, and I wouldn't want to. (Okay, I would, but I won't.)"

## Spiritual Lessons for Life Path 5

These are the rule-breakers, the crowd-stirrers, the ones who can't just read the menu; they want to taste everything on it. Preferably in multiple countries. With local spice.

Ironically, the soul lesson of a 5 is not to escape life, but to fully engage with it. To discover that freedom isn't about running away, but about choosing how to stay. They are here to learn how to balance change with consistency, stimulation with serenity, and chaos with clarity. They often grow through contrast: wild adventures followed by periods of intense grounding. The universe keeps trying to hand them a map, and they keep turning it into an origami swan. Eventually, though, the 5 will discover that structure doesn't kill freedom, it protects it.

When a 5 finds their purpose and commits to a path (with enough wiggle room, of course), they become powerful communicators, activists, artists, leaders, and yes, life partners. Their energy becomes magnetic rather than scattered. They don't stop moving but start moving with intention.

**From a Life Path 5's perspective. Their perfect partner:**

Great Match. Easy flow, natural understanding; 1, 5, and 11.

Good Match. Supportive, friendly, promising; 3, 9, and 7.

Ambitious Match. Full of potential but needs work; 2, 4, 6, 22, and 33.

A Neutral Match. Could go either way, depends on maturity, and interests; 8, and 44.

6

# Life Path 6: Built to Love, Wired to Worry

A master of casseroles, guilt trips, and beautifully over-functioning in everyone else's life: "I've already taken care of that, you're welcome".

6s are the people who bring cupcakes to a PTA meeting they didn't attend. They've got a to-do list for your life, and you didn't even ask. Compassionate, organized, and two steps ahead of everyone emotionally, that is, until they burn out and wonder why no one appreciates their silent suffering. These folks are natural caretakers, bleeding hearts, and professional advice-givers who will die on the hill of "I just want what's best for you." Also: they secretly resent being everyone's emotional support human… but good luck getting them to admit it.

In love and friendship, a 6 gives you everything: rides to the airport, home-cooked meals, and highly detailed suggestions on how you should make your decisions. (Spoiler, their idea is the best, so, just sayin'). They love deeply and thoroughly, often with hand-drawn diagrams of your potential. But their generosity has strings, usually embroidered with passive-aggressive guilt and tied in a bow of "I'm just trying to help." They don't want to be controlling, but also, you're doing it wrong.

Their emotional range deserves a canvas. Or a novel. Or a blog that doubles as group therapy. Creative outlets are essential for a 6's sanity, and lucky for us, their sensitivity is a gold mine for honest, meaningful art that makes people cry in public. You've got the rare ability to manage conflict and still be liked afterward. A 6 will believe in you when you don't believe in yourself. They will praise you for things no other person noticed ("I love how you organized the Post-its by mood!") and may offer unsolicited life coaching over lunch. Their default setting is supportive mentor, which is beautiful until you try to push a deadline, and they say, "I'm not mad. I'm just disappointed."

When their halo slips, a 6 doesn't go dark; they go dramatic martyr. The shadow 6 can be judgy, controlling, and clingy, but always with a "loving" tone. If you've ever been guilted into gratitude or complimented in a way that feels oddly like a warning, congrats, you've met an unbalanced 6. They enable toxic behavior while resenting it, use self-sacrifice as social currency, and somehow weaponize kindness. Emotional manipulation? Only if you count tears, sighs, and the phrase, "After everything I've done for you."

As much as they talk about teamwork, 6s are deeply suspicious of anyone doing things "wrong" (meaning: not their way). So, they tend to micromanage through smiling teeth. They mean well, but will 100% burn out while smiling and saying, "It's fine, I've got it."

## How to Spot a 6 in the Wild

They look like a hug… and also like they're silently judging your shoes.

You won't always see a 6 coming, but you'll definitely feel their energy settle into the room like a weighted blanket with a plan. There's something stabilizing about them, even if they're just standing in line for tacos. They give off the quiet vibe of someone who could mediate a family crisis and fix your phone screen in one afternoon.

**Their posture?** Relaxed but intentional. 6s rarely slouch or sprawl. They carry themselves like someone who's already thought through their exit strategy to keep you safe if trouble arises and would absolutely have brought their umbrella in case of a thunderstorm, without making a big deal about it.

**Calm movements.** Thay are capable, and quietly in charge. They don't flail, pace, or fiddle. They move with purpose, even if that purpose is just finding the best seat for optimal conversation flow. When they sit down, it feels like someone just dimmed the emotional noise in the room by 40%.

**Unofficial guardian of the group vibe.** They're the ones who remembered extra napkins, double-checked the directions, and noticed you looked a little off. They don't hover, but they see everything. If someone's missing, they text. If someone's hurting, they offer actual help, real help, not just a hug and a quote from Instagram.

**You can talk to me.** 6s have an expression that hovers somewhere between thoughtful curiosity and low-key concern. Their smile is real, not forced, and it often shows up before you've said anything. They don't just listen; they absorb. You'll feel oddly compelled to open up about your strained sibling relationship or your vitamin D levels.

**Orderly sense of style.** Whether they lean toward stylish decor, modern minimalist, or cozy-but-capable chic, there's usually a sense of order in how they present themselves. They're not flashy, but they look like they respect themselves and their calendar. Bonus points if their jacket has an emergency granola bar in the pocket.

**Eyes look warm, alert, and a little tired.** Not from lack of sleep, but from carrying everyone's emotional baggage up the stairs. When a 6 looks at you, it's like being scanned by a therapist, an EMT, and a barista who genuinely cares.

In short: If someone offers you a ride, a solution, and a reminder to call your mom, all before the appetizers arrive, you've probably met a 6.

**BONUS CLUES:**

They carry tissues, gum, and someone else's phone charger, just in case.

They smell faintly of essential oils and responsibility.

They complement your potential, not just your outfit.

They say things like "I just want everyone to feel included," and mean it.

## The Dating Style of a 6

Dating a 6 is like stepping into a warm, cozy blanket fort... that they built for you before the second date. They're charmingly romantic, loyal to a fault, and just a little too eager to meet your parents. Their idea of flirting might involve offering to do your taxes or emotionally resuscitating your inner child. Whether you're ready or not, this person is planning for "our" future, and I hope you like handmade holiday cards.

When you first meet a 6, you'll be struck by how genuinely kind they are. They listen. They care. They remember your dog's name and ask about your cousin's surgery. You'll wonder if it's a trap. It's not. They're just built this way. They show up ready to emotionally commit before your second cocktail arrives.

They love hard. They show up. They organize your spice rack while you're in the shower. They offer to help you update your resume. Suddenly, you're wondering if this is love or an intervention. The 6 courtship style is full-on, expect sweet gestures, deep talks, and a subtle attempt to become the project manager of your emotional healing.

Be careful, you may look up one day and realize you've lost your autonomy in a sea of well-meaning caretaking. You can't sneeze without someone handing you tea and signing you up for allergy testing. If they're unbalanced, a 6 will turn every dinner conversation into a topic about the future. They mean well. But also... blink twice if you feel emotionally smothered.

## Dating Style of a 6: Masculine Edition

The 6 man doesn't come in swinging with flashy lines or dramatic entrances. He shows up. On time. With plans. And possibly cheese, crackers, and a bottle of good wine. His version of romance isn't about mystery; it's about stability, effort, and making sure your tire pressure is correct before a road trip. He leads with loyalty and quiet strength, not ego. While others might try to impress with bravado, the 6 man wins hearts by making you feel protected, seen, and supported, without making it weird. He's not trying to be a hero. He's trying to be your person.

He may not say a lot at first, but he's paying attention. If you mention something offhand, regarding your favorite restaurant, that your dog hates thunderstorms, or that your boss is being awful, he'll store it in his mental file labeled "Important." The next time a storm rolls in? He's at your door with noise-canceling headphones and your favorite takeout.

When it comes to dating gestures, think:

Planning dates that consider your preferences and comfort.

Carrying heavy things without being showy.

Offering advice not to dominate, but because he genuinely wants to help.

He is a protector, not a preacher. He's got strong opinions, but he won't bulldoze yours. He's often the guy friends go to when their world falls apart, and when he loves someone, he makes sure they don't have to fall apart alone.

He has old-school values with modern emotional intelligence. He will want to pay for dinner, open doors, and make sure you get home safe, but he'll also apologize when he's wrong, check in on your mental health, and never ghost you like some chaotic Life Paths. (No offense, 5).

He flirts with consistency and care, and while he may not lead with poetry, he's the kind of guy who will hold you through the hard stuff, keep showing up, and never stop trying to make life feel a little easier, a little safer, and a lot more rooted.

## What Flirting Looks Like from a 6.

Flirting with a 6 isn't always easy to spot, mostly because it looks suspiciously like caregiving, low-stakes therapy, or helping you put together IKEA furniture "just for fun." But trust me, if a 6 is into you, you'll know. They don't come in hot. They come in helpful.

They'll offer to walk your dog, drive you to the airport, or fix your wobbly chair. Not because they're trying to score points, but because they already see you as someone worth investing in. For a 6, flirting equals gentle consistency. If they like you, they'll keep showing up... in increasingly thoughtful and slightly adorable ways.

That intense but kind steady eye contact when you're talking. They're not just listening. They're taking mental notes about your allergies, your dreams, and your favorite kind of soup. "I just happened to bring extra". Whether it's gum, gloves, or emotional support snacks, they've got it for you. And no, they didn't just happen to bring it.

Mini check-ins. "Did you eat today?" "How did that meeting go?" "Need help with that thing you mentioned three weeks ago?" This isn't casual kindness. This is their version of "I'm really into you, and also I might lowkey love your dog." Less wink and smirk, more "You okay? You sure? I brought tea just in case." Less mystery and seduction, more "Here's a heating pad and your favorite cake. Now tell me who hurt you."

If they love you, you'll start noticing small upgrades in your life. Your plants thrive. Your bookshelf gets alphabetized. You somehow start drinking more water and filing your taxes early. This isn't a coincidence, it's the quiet magic of a 6 making your world more livable... because they care. Just know that if they're investing time, attention, and practical acts of love in you... that is the flirt.

**DO:**

**Do be emotionally available.** And open to deep conversations.

**Do appreciate the tiny details**. They're paying attention.

**Do ask them how they're doing**. They forget to check in with themselves.

**Do encourage them to not fix everything.** Including you.

**DON'T:**

**Don't take their kindness for granted**. They'll pretend it's fine but silently grow some passive-aggressive attitudes inside.

**Don't dismiss their emotional concerns**. They've been holding them in for weeks.

**Don't get lazy in the relationship**, and they'll pick up the slack and resent you forever.

**A few Affirmations if Dating a 6:**

To be read aloud while holding hands, making eye contact, and agreeing to eventually adopt another dog.

"I am deeply grateful for your constant, over-functioning love."

"Your emotional support is not required, but respected."

"I can do things on my own. (I'll text you when I get there.")

"You are not my therapist, my life coach, or my mom. You're my partner."

"Boundaries make us sexy."

"You don't have to earn love. You just get to be loved."

**Spiritual Lessons: Help Others, But Please Sit Down**

The soul lesson for a Life Path 6 is loving without losing themselves. They must learn that being supportive does not mean being in charge. That it's okay to say no, and okay to let people learn things the hard way, even if it makes them itch inside. Their challenge is to stop parenting everyone and start trusting the universe not to drop the baby.

6 is comforting, warm, and occasionally too much. They're fierce defenders of the people they love and perfectionists about how love should look. When at their best, they're the glue that holds the family, the group chat, and your entire nervous system together.

**From a Life Path 6s perspective. Their perfect partner:**

Great Match. Easy flow, natural understanding; 6, 9, and 33.

Good Match. Supportive, friendly, promising; 2, 4, 8, 22, and 44.

Ambitious Match. Full of potential but needs work; 1, 5, 7, and 11.

A Neutral Match. Could go either way, depends on maturity; 3.

# Life Path 7: The Enlightened Hermit

If 6 was the cosmic caretaker, 7 is the brooding genius hiding in the observatory, journaling about why emotions are suspicious. These are the people who feel everything but will spend six weeks analyzing the pros and cons of texting you back. They're deep, cerebral, and allergic to small talk.

They're philosophers disguised as accountants. Mystics who can build spreadsheets. Solitary seekers of truth who secretly judge your TV choices. And while they might seem cold on the outside, inside is a swirling galaxy of emotion, suspicion, and spiritual wonder... neatly categorized in a mental filing cabinet.

7s have run a full background check on their souls. They are intellectual snobs, but the lovable kind. They read books about books. They ask questions that start with "But what is the truth of that and then go quiet for three days while meditating on the answer. They often work alone, need a lot of recharge time, and are most comfortable in deep research, spiritual inquiry, or silent judgment. Their intuition is off the charts. They have a knack for reading between the lines, catching subtle details most people miss, and making sense of complicated situations without getting lost in the noise.

"I'm not avoiding you; I'm just investigating the nature of reality… alone… with noise-canceling headphones." They don't mean to be antisocial. They're just trying to solve the mysteries of existence in peace. If you interrupt them mid-thought, they will either blink slowly… or mentally erase you.

Getting close to a 7 takes time. You don't "click" with them; you pass a series of spiritual, intellectual, and emotional gatekeeping challenges. Once inside, they're loyal, insightful, and can love deeply, but you'll have to accept that their love language might be "I fixed your Wi-Fi and found your soul's purpose."

They need space. Lots of it. They hate drama, demand truth, and prefer authentic silence to polite conversation. Don't try to "crack them open", just be real, and let them hand you keys one at a time. Or don't. They're fine either way.

They are operating from their higher self, it's like being around a quiet storm of wisdom and wit. They're calm and focused, rarely rattled by chaos, and they bring a kind of steady energy that makes people instinctively trust them. At first glance, they may seem reserved, even serious, but give them time to warm up and you'll discover their secret weapon: a dry, unexpected humor that sneaks up on you in the middle of a profound conversation about the meaning of life.

**The shadow of the 7:**

When off balance, 7s becomes the emotionally unavailable philosopher king. Their high standards and obsessive analysis turn into rigid judgment, perfectionism, and general hatred, distrust, or dislike of humankind. They start believing no one understands them (sometimes true), no one is trustworthy (less true), and that everything meaningful must be found alone in a field during a lunar eclipse.

They can be: Hypercritical (especially of themselves), withdrawn, unapproachable, and suspicious of others' motives.

And this one can be tricky. 7s can be emotionally aloof with a superiority complex wrapped in a blanket of spiritual bypassing. 7's are granted more spiritual information than the rest of us, and that could make them so "spiritual" they end up being of no earthly use. Let them be. They'll come around if they notice no one is listening anymore.

**How to Spot a 7 in the Wild.**

7s are not easy to spot, mainly because they tend to avoid being seen. These folks blend into their surroundings like philosophical chameleons, scanning the room for meaning, subtle hypocrisy, and the quickest exit. Their vibe is calm, controlled, and completely unreadable, until they decide otherwise.

If a 6 radiates warmth and a 5 radiates chaos, the 7 radiates "Don't touch my aura, thanks." Their facial expressions are mysterious, and they often look like they just finished reading a metaphysical text that ruined their entire day (but in a good way).

**A 7 doesn't fidget.** They hover in place like a sentient stone sculpture. They're the person in a crowded room who's not moving, not talking, and not making eye contact, unless engaged in a conversation of profound consequence for life or the planet. Even though they are busy, they are still observing everything. You'll feel their presence before they speak. If they do speak, everyone else shuts up.

When they finally make a hand gesture, you'd better pay attention, because it was intentional. 7s don't do jazz hands. They do slow, deliberate hand movements that suggest they're guiding you through the multiverse, or about to deliver a plot twist.

**The Gaze That Sees Through Lies and Possibly Dimensions.**

Their eye contact is intense. Not aggressive, but penetrating. You'll want to look away but also confess your deepest fears. Their eyes say, "I already know your secrets".

**Self-Contained, Privacy-First Posture.**

7s wrap themselves in their own energy field. Crossed arms, closed-off body angles, a slight lean away from your chaos, they're not being rude. They're filtering in life through 17 layers of analysis and trauma-informed observation. If they uncross their arms, congrats, you're in!

**Deliberate, Thoughtful Movement.** If they ever move quickly, it's either a fire alarm or someone accidentally misquoted Carl Jung. You won't hear them shouting across a room. Their voice is measured, quiet, and borderline hypnotic. You lean in not just to hear them, but because their tone sounds like it might contain a hidden message. Spoiler: it does. And it will change how you view your childhood. You didn't even notice them until they spoke, and then you questioned your entire life.

**Bonus clues.**

They're sitting near a window. With a journal. And probably judging your loud conversation.

They're the only ones not checking their phone. They hate phones.

Their facial expression says "fascinated" and "I need to leave soon" at the same time.

You can feel them listening... from across the room.

Awkward genius meets emotional mystery, with a side of "Yes, I like you, but please don't call me before noon."

**The Dating Style of a 7.** "I Like You. But From Over There. Quietly."

Dating a 7 is like signing up for an advanced course in emotional archaeology. You won't get swept off your feet, but you might get swept into a three-hour conversation about consciousness, quantum theory, or the spiritual symbolism of mushrooms. And enjoy it.

They're thoughtful, mysterious, and so emotionally reserved they make Victorian furniture look loose and casual. But once you're "in," you've earned a partner with insane depth, quiet solid loyalty, and a surprisingly kinky imagination (it will show up eventually).

They'll never love-bomb you, but they will send you links to obscure articles and then wait anxiously to see if you understood them. Romance, to a 7, is mind-first, body-second, feelings-someday. You'll talk philosophy before touching hands, and if they bring you into their sacred space (and let you stay past their solitude window), you've officially made the cut.

**In shadow?** They'll disappear to recharge, analyze your texts like sacred scrolls, and struggle to express their emotions unless you give them lots of space and zero pressure. Push too hard? They ghost. Stay too shallow? They lose interest. Your best bet: be real, be calm, and be weird enough to intrigue them.

## Dating Style of a 7: Masculine Edition

As you'll notice reading this section, the personality style while dating is, for the most part, the same if dating a man or a woman 7. Just like a woman a man dates like a philosopher. He's quiet, composed, and observant, less about charm, more about depth. You won't get flashy gestures or oversharing on the first date. Instead, he'll ask a question so specific it feels like he's already read your soul. 7s don't fall fast; they study you, learning your patterns before revealing their own. He's self-contained, spiritually curious, and emotionally precise. When he lets you in, it's intentional and rare. But if you earn his trust, you'll have a fiercely loyal partner who protects your solitude, respects your intelligence, and makes you feel like the only real thing in a very confusing world.

## When A 7 is Flirting:

If a 7 is flirting with you, you may not realize it right away. You'll just start to feel... observed. Not in a creepy way (okay, a little creepy if you're not used to it), but in a "why do I suddenly want to confess my deepest fears and Google metaphysics?" kind of way.

7s just don't flirt in the traditional sense. You won't get a wink or a bold pickup line. Instead, they'll stare at you across the room with unnerving intensity, then later approach to casually ask your opinion on consciousness or whether time is linear. They're not here for small talk. They're here for soul, world, society, higher education, and science-y talk. In general, 7s thrive in academia, so if you have a subject you're passionate about and have studied deeply, they'll only have eyes (and time) for you.

Flirting to them is sharing obscure spiritual or scientific facts like, "Did you know octopuses have nine brains?", then watching your reaction very carefully to determine if you may be the one. They may say: "You liked that movie? Interesting". And then want to sit down and unpack your entire worldview.

They may flirt by inviting you to something strange, low-key, and mystical, like a meditation hike, a sound bath, or maybe a coffee to glean all you know that they may not have heard of yet. Spoiler... It's not likely you will have anything completely new to them, but they'll be intrigued AF if you bring it.

**And if a 7 really likes you? They will:**

Give you a book that changed their life.

Some may ask for your birth time (not for astrology, but to run your full karmic blueprint).

Quietly Google whether your Life Path is compatible with theirs. (They will not tell you they did this, but now they know that you know, because they will have absolutely read this book, just sayin').

They don't want a fling. They want a soulmate who understands their inner labyrinth and won't panic when they disappear for three days to process a feeling. So, if someone's making you question reality, recommending Pythagoras's way of counting numbers over cocktails, and keeps "accidentally" brushing your hand while explaining parallel dimensions? Congratulations. A 7 is definitely flirting with you.

So, You Couldn't Help Yourself, You've Fallen for a 7 …

**DO:**

**Do be genuinely curious.** Ask weird questions. Bring depth.

**Do respect their need for space.** Emotional, physical, and galactic.

**Do share ideas.** Not just feelings. Intellectual conversation *is* foreplay.

**Do be authentic.** They can sniff out fakery before you finish a sentence.

**Do let silence be sacred.** Not awkward.

**DON'T:**

**Don't smother them.** They'll vanish like mist.

**Don't try to "fix" their silence.** It's not broken; it's planned.

**Don't expect them to talk** about feelings on demand.

**Don't overshare early on.** They need time to build emotional bandwidth.

**Don't mistake their distance for disinterest.** If they're still texting, they're in.

**Emergency Affirmations When Dating a 7:**

**For those moments when you're spiraling because they didn't use an emoji.**

"I am not being ghosted. They're in hermit mode."

"Depth takes time. This isn't fast food, it's slow-simmered soul stew."

"Just because they didn't say it doesn't mean they're not feeling it."

"They didn't text for two days. That's practically affectionate."

"Their silence is a compliment. They don't waste words on just anyone."

"I'm not losing them. They're recharging from human contact."

"They showed me their bookshelf. That's the 7 version of a love poem."

"It's not cold. It's contemplative."

**Spiritual Lessons of the Life Path 7**

The soul of a 7 came here to master the art of trust, both in themselves and in something bigger than themselves. Their spiritual lesson isn't about gathering endless knowledge; it's about transforming knowledge into wisdom. They're here to learn that life's mysteries aren't solved by logic alone, but by balancing intuition with intellect, solitude with connection, and questions with faith.

7s are natural seekers, but part of their path is realizing they don't have to isolate to find the answers. They're learning to open up, to let others in on their journey instead of disappearing into the wilderness of their own minds. Their growth comes from discovering that vulnerability doesn't weaken their insight; it deepens it.

The 7 is here to integrate head and heart. To learn that knowing the truth is not the same as living it. That intuition isn't just found in silence; it's felt in connection. Their soul is learning how to trust, to feel without fear, and to come down from the mental mountaintop once in a while and, *gasp*, talk to people.

And what do they teach the rest of us? To slow down. To listen. To look beyond the surface and trust the quiet voice inside that knows the way. 7s remind us that introspection isn't avoidance, it's a sacred space for understanding who we are and why we're here. Through their example, we learn that real wisdom isn't about knowing everything; it's about knowing what truly matters. They have an uncanny ability to help others find clarity, not by telling you what to think, but by asking the questions that make you realize you've had the answers all along.

**So, if you're a 7?**

You're not alone, not really.

Now go take a nap. Or read three books. Or both.

The world will still be full of mysteries tomorrow.

**From a Life Path 7s perspective. Their perfect partner:**

Great Match. Easy flow, natural understanding;  5, 7, and 22.

Good Match. Supportive, friendly, promising; 1, 4, and 11.

Ambitious Match. Full of potential but needs work; 2, 3, 6, 9, and 33.

A Neutral Match. Could go either way, depends on maturity; 8, and 44.

# Life Path 8: The Powerhouse in Designer Shoes

Ambition is the vibe. Excellence is the standard. Control is... inevitable.

The 8 walks into a room like they've already decided whether or not to invest in it. These individuals don't dream; they strategize. The 8 wakes up already in fifth gear. They negotiate while brushing their teeth, conquer before breakfast, and still remind you that your handshake is weak. They're disciplined, decisive, and allergic to mediocrity. Expect big goals, bigger follow-through, and the occasional motivational quote that sounds vaguely threatening ("Dream big or get out of my way").

They don't believe in luck, only leverage, and they live by a self-written rulebook titled "How to Win Without Apologizing for It." People often admire their focus and drive. They feel most secure when they are in control of their environment, and occasionally, yours.

When young, teachers called them "strong-willed," classmates called them "bossy," and the principal called them "future board member." They take themselves seriously from an early age, often feeling a strange sense of responsibility long before it's required. They are early bloomers when it comes to understanding how influence works.

8s approach relationships with the same energy they bring to building empires: steady, strategic, and fully committed once they're in. They're fiercely loyal, protective, and want to know you're bringing your best self to the table, not perfection, but effort. Their love isn't about constant fireworks or gushy declarations; it's about showing up, growing together, and achieving big goals side by side.

8s won't shower you in endless romantic fluff, they'll do something better: they'll have your back. If chaos hits, they won't panic; they'll grab a whiteboard and draw up a recovery plan. They prefer solutions to sympathy and are allergic to unnecessary drama, translation: they will love you, but they will also question why you're crying over a late DoorDash order.

Vulnerability isn't their first language, not because they don't feel deeply, but because they like emotions that work with them, not ones that derail progress. Understand and support them in this? Congratulations, you've passed a series of secret internal evaluations, and they now trust you not to waste their time or break their heart.

8

8s are the builders, protectors, and powerhouses of the numerology world. They're ambitious and fiercely loyal, bringing a mix of stability and drive to every relationship they enter. Dating an 8 means being with someone who wants to grow together, not just emotionally, but in life goals, security, and mutual respect. They love deeply but practically; their version of romance is showing up, following through, and making sure you're taken care of in ways you didn't even know you needed.

Yes, they can be intense. Their twilight side can slip into control-freak territory, and they're known to occasionally bulldoze feelings in the name of progress. But at their best? They're generous, protective partners who will stand by you through anything. They're not here for half-hearted love; they want something real, lasting, and built to endure. If you can handle their strength, and remind them that vulnerability doesn't equal weakness, you'll find that behind every 8s drive is a heart that just wants someone worth building a life with.

**The surprising shadow of the 8.**

On paper, 8s look like they've got it all figured out: confident, ambitious, magnetic. People assume they're financially set, or at least well on their way to becoming the next mogul. But here's the twist: I've met more broke 8s than rich ones. Why? Because that same confidence that fuels their ambition can also make them unusually comfortable with risk. Big leaps, bold moves, all-in bets, they're willing to gamble on themselves in ways other numbers wouldn't dare. Sometimes it pays off. Sometimes… not so much.

The natural charisma, the leadership energy, even the knack for looking polished (or at least wearing the illusion of polished). They may discover early on that confidence and, yes, the proper suit labels, can open doors. But real, lasting success, in both love and money, requires something more: grounded decisions and clear-eyed awareness of the facts.

**How to Spot a 8 in the Wild.** (Warning: Do not attempt to out-alpha them. You will lose.)

If you find yourself suddenly standing up straighter, adjusting your tie, or rethinking your life goals, congrats! You've likely wandered into the magnetic force field of an 8. These individuals do not blend in. They walk like the room belongs to them, stand like they've just closed a multimillion-dollar deal, and talk like they already know your five-year plan (and could probably improve it). Spotting them isn't hard; you'll feel their energy before they even speak. But just in case you're unsure, here's your cheat sheet:

**Confident posture?** Always. 8s don't slouch. Slouching is for people with unresolved potential. You'll see them standing tall with their shoulders back like a corporate warrior ready to launch into battle, or a motivational keynote, whichever comes first.

**Purposeful movement?** Every step they take feels like a mission. You won't catch them wandering aimlessly or strolling, they stride. If they drop something, they pick it up like it was all planned. If they enter a room, they do so as if they're announcing quarterly profits.

**Steady, unblinking eye contact?** Yep. Not aggressive, but definitely firm enough to make you sit up straighter and remember all the boundaries you should've kept. These folks lock eyes like they're confirming a contract, because, honestly, they probably are.

**Strong, deliberate gestures?** 8s speak with their hands, but not flailing, jazz-hands-style. Think: slicing the air to emphasize a point, pointing to the future (literally), or calmly clasping their hands like they're solving the problems of capitalism.

**Controlled body language?** Oh yes. Every move they make has been pre-approved by the inner boardroom. You won't see fidgeting or hesitation. If their arms are crossed, it's not insecurity; it's a power stance. If they tilt their head, it means you've said something interesting, or dangerously incorrect.

**Authoritative tone?** Let's just say they don't "suggest." They "recommend with finality." Even their compliments sound like promotions ("You've really grown into your potential, Mike. Proud of you. Now let's double those results").

So, if someone walks into your space, sets the tempo of the room, and makes you want to raise your standards? You're looking at an 8 in the wild. Offer them a strong handshake, speak with purpose, and for heaven's sake, don't waste their time.

## Dating Style of a 8

Dating an 8 is like dating someone who already knows where they're going and wants to see if you're ready to go there too. They bring the same energy to relationships that they bring to building empires: focused, intentional, and built for the long haul. Their love language? Loyalty, commitment, and making sure the rent is paid on time.

At first, they might seem a little intense. 8s don't usually "play it cool," they are cool, but they're also scanning for signs that you're trustworthy, self-sufficient, and willing to grow with them. They want a partner, not a project. If you bring drama, they'll offer solutions. If you bring consistency, they'll match it with protection and devotion.

First dates might happen at networking mixers, investor lunches, or a quick stop by their office, so you can see what they've built. Flowers are lovely, but if you want to impress an 8, show up on time, bring ideas, and for the love of gold-plated spreadsheets, don't be flaky. They're not looking for someone to complete them; they're looking for someone to scale with. Expect a mix of "How was your day?" and "Let's launch a brand together." They show love through action: planning, fixing, and improving. If they send you a PDF titled "Joint Budget Forecast," that's basically a proposal. They look like they just walked off the set of Shark Tank, and they're here to pitch themselves and evaluate your potential. Dress sharp. Speak clearly. And remember, confidence is currency.

## Dating Style of a 8: Masculine Edition

The 8 man dates like he negotiates life, directly, confidently, and with long-term goals in mind. He's not here to dabble; he's looking for a partner who can stand beside him, not behind him. He thrives on ambition and respects people who know what they want. If you bring purpose to the table, you'll have his full attention. If you bring chaos, he'll hand you an action plan… or quietly show you the door. He shows affection through protection and provision. This is the guy who fixes things before you notice they're broken, makes sure your car is winterized, and buys the good wine (because he can and because you deserve it). His flirting style? Confident eye contact, intentional compliments, and the subtle flex of someone who's got his life handled, even if he's still figuring out the details.

An 8 in love is protective and deeply reliable. They'll remember you like to sleep till 9 on weekends, and handle the big-picture stuff that makes life easier. But don't expect endless romantic fluff or spontaneous poetry; they show love through action. If they fix it, build it, or make it happen for you, that is their version of "I love you."

Their need for control can sometimes sneak into dating. They like things done right (translation: their way), and vulnerability doesn't come easily. But if they let you in, past the armor, you'll find someone whose loyalty runs deep and whose love is as enduring as their ambition. He doesn't fall fast, but when he does, he's all in. Loyalty, consistency, and building a future together, that's his love language.

## When They Flirt:

An 8 man doesn't flirt the way most people do, no cheesy pick-up lines, no exaggerated charm. His flirting style is direct, confident, and purposeful. You'll know he's interested because he says so, or because he's already planning the next date before dessert arrives.

He's the type to lean in close when you're talking, make unwavering eye contact, and drop a compliment so specific you're not sure whether to blush or take notes. ("That color you're wearing? It makes your eyes look like they're plotting world domination.")

Instead of constant texts, he'll call, because his time is valuable, and so is yours. He might tease you lightly, but never cruelly; his humor is confident, never needy. And if he really likes you? He'll quietly start handling things: making sure you're safe when you leave, grabbing the check without fanfare, or subtly protecting you from life's little hassles, because in his mind, that's romance.

Warning: If an 8 is into you, he'll test you, gently. Can you handle his ambition? His schedule? His high standards? If yes, you've earned his respect, and trust me: once an 8 commits, they're in it for the long haul.

**If you've let yourself fall in love with an 8**

**DO:**

**Do match their ambition.** You don't need to be a CEO, but you should know what you want in life and actively pursue it. They admire drive.

**Do respect their time.** 8s are busy building an empire (or at least a stable future). Show up when you say you will.

**Do appreciate their protection.** They like taking care of the people they love, not because they think you can't, but because they want to.

**Do communicate directly.** If something's wrong, say it. They don't do well with guessing games or mixed signals. They don't play the "Come and get me" game. At least not for long.

**Do celebrate their wins.** Acknowledge their efforts; they thrive on recognition from those closest to them, because those close to them are deeply respected.

**DON'T:**

**Don't play mind games.** They'll see right through them and won't stick around for the drama.

**Don't mistake confidence for arrogance.** They are intense, not heartless. Learn the difference before you misjudge them.

**Don't undermine their vision, their goals.** Criticism without support will feel like betrayal to them.

**Don't ignore the practical side of life.** Bills, responsibilities, and long-term planning, if you act like these don't matter, you'll begin to not matter.

**Don't assume they're bulletproof.** Beneath that strong exterior is someone who feels deeply. Handle with care.

**Affirmations for Dating an 8**

"Their strength doesn't overshadow me; it supports me."

"I can match their drive without losing my own peace."

"Their ambition is not a threat; it's an invitation to grow together."

"I appreciate their need for structure without feeling controlled."

"I bring calm to their storm, and they bring focus to my chaos."

"I respect their goals, and they respect my heart."

"We build trust by communicating openly, not silently guessing."

"I know their love shows up in actions, even when words are scarce."

"I don't need to compete with their independence; I can celebrate it."

## Spiritual Lessons:

Most important, power without heart is just noise…

The soul lesson for a Life Path 8 is all about mastering power without becoming a prisoner to it. These individuals are here to learn that true strength comes not from control, but from balance. Their journey is about learning when to lead and when to trust, when to speak and when to listen, when to hustle, and when to let go. They are often tested through success, money, authority, and ego, and the universe will lovingly (or not-so-lovingly) remind them that compassion and connection are part of the package as well. When they integrate emotional intelligence with their natural leadership, they become unstoppable forces for good, building not just empires but legacies.

8s are here to dominate, innovate, and elevate. They are the CEOs of their lives, the strategists of their dreams, and the people who make things happen when others are still making excuses. But beneath all that power is a deeply complex soul learning how to be both strong and soft, both driven and grounded. When balanced, they are empowering leaders who uplift those around them. When out of balance, they become cautionary tales of burnout, pride, or cold ambition. Either way, their path is never small, never dull, and always moving toward greatness, preferably ahead of schedule.

And when an 8 loves someone, it's because they trust them on many levels, emotionally, mentally, and even spiritually. They don't hand over their heart lightly, so when they do, you know it's real. Having an 8 as a partner means you've got someone who will stand by you in every storm, protect what you're building together, and believe in your potential as fiercely as their own.

**From a Life Path 8s perspective. Their perfect partner:**

Great Match. Easy flow, natural understanding; 2, 4, 8, 22, and 44.

Good Match. Supportive, friendly, promising; 3, 6, and 9.

Ambitious Match. Full of potential but needs work; 5, 7, and 11.

A Neutral Match. Could go either way, depends on maturity; 1, and 33.

# 9

# Life Path 9: The Old Soul with a Passport to Every Lifetime

If all the Life Paths were cast in a movie, the 9 would be the world-weary legacy builder who's seen it all, felt it all, and still shows up with organic granola bars and a donation form. 9s are the empathic, creative visionaries of numerology, the ones most likely to cry during a documentary and create their own community nonprofit before dessert. They're generous to a fault, insightful to the bone, and somehow manage to remember your dog's birthday better than their own.

But before we light incense and put on the Enya, let's get into it.

As a kid, little 9s are wise beyond their years. These are the kids asking philosophical questions during snack time: "Why do bad things happen to good people?" as everyone else is stuffing Cheez-Its in their faces. They care deeply about fairness, animals, and whether or not that goldfish really went to heaven. You might find them comforting a sad classmate, painting emotional masterpieces with finger paint, or refusing to throw away a broken toy "because it still has feelings." They're natural helpers but sometimes take on way more than a child should.

By the time a 9 hits adulthood, they've usually accumulated enough emotional baggage to open an airport lost-luggage warehouse. But instead of stewing in it, they alchemize it into compassion. They're driven by a deep need to make the world better, whether that means hugging it out, hosting a charity auction, or just giving a stranger a ride to the shelter because "something told them to." Their natural intuition is freakishly on point. They know you're about to cancel plans before you do, and they've already forgiven you for it. But they also carry an invisible weight, a quiet sadness that comes from feeling like they're never doing quite enough. (Spoiler: They are.)

Friendships with a 9 can feel like emotional spa days. They listen like therapists and give advice like fortune cookies dipped in honey. However, their *need* to help can morph into *overhelping*, and you may find yourself saying, "I just wanted to vent, not get a full intervention."

They're wonderful to have in your corner... unless you're a narcissist, in which case they will mystically disappear from your life (or get sucked into trying to save you for 10 years before waking up one day and deleting your number mid-meditation).

**The shadow side of our 9's**

For all their light, 9s can wander into some surprisingly dark corners, usually while wearing a halo. Their shadow often disguises itself as virtue: over-giving until they collapse, sacrificing for people who never asked, or quietly judging those who don't meet their lofty ideals.

Their passive-aggression? Olympic level. They won't raise their voice, but you'll feel the guilt radiate off them like incense smoke. And when they ghost, it's rarely because they don't care, it's because they care too much and don't know how to stay without absorbing every ounce of your emotional baggage.

The good news? This shadow stems from a big heart that's still learning to strike a balance. Once they realize they don't have to save everyone (just the ones who actually want saving), their compassion becomes a gift instead of a burden.

## How to Spot a 9 in the Wild

(Hint: They're probably comforting a stranger, rescuing a stray animal, or passionately explaining how love will save the world.)

You'll rarely find a 9 hunched over a spreadsheet or aggressively networking at a cocktail party. No, these radiant humanitarians are the ones making deep eye contact with the barista, slipping a $10 bill into a stranger's parking meter, or tearing up during a community art project. Spotting one in the wild isn't hard, if you know what to look for.

**Open arms, open heart.**

9s rarely cross their arms. Why? Because they're always ready to hug. Their body language is relaxed, open, and welcoming, as if they're saying, "Come tell me your trauma. I made tea."

**Empathetic eye contact.**

When a 9 looks at you, it's like being seen by an old soul who knows the lyrics to your childhood wounds. They really look at you. Like, "I know you're saying you're fine, but your aura says otherwise" kind of looking.

**Expressive gestures.**

Talking to a 9 can feel like watching a one-person stage play. Their hands fly around, their face emotes everything, and they're not afraid to act out the part of "the downtrodden masses" if it helps make a point.

From their smile to the way they touch your arm while reassuring you, a 9 radiates that warm, squishy vibe you usually only get from grandmothers and golden retrievers. You don't just feel safe, you feel understood.

**Idealistic as ever.**

Listen for someone saying things like, "I just believe we can create a world where everyone is fed and emotionally fulfilled." That's a 9. They speak in big visions, healing dreams, and slightly unrealistic (but deeply heartfelt) blueprints for global change.

Relaxed posture with a dash of worldly weight.

They look laid-back on the outside, but if you squint, you'll notice the faint shadow of crisis just behind their peaceful smile. They're relaxed, but also carrying the emotional burdens of three continents.

## A 9s Dating Style

(Loves long walks on the beach, ideally while organizing a beach clean-up.)

Dating a 9 is like stepping into a romantic indie film… one with a social justice subplot and an acoustic soundtrack. These are the bleeding hearts of the numerology world, the passionate visionaries who feel your pain, your dog's pain, and possibly the emotional legacy of your ancestral lineage. They fall hard, not always wisely, but definitely completely. When they fall for you, you might be surprised to receive a love note, a book of Rumi poems, and a list of volunteer opportunities that align with your shared core values.

9s often come across as soulful, warm, and slightly overwhelmed by how much love they have to give the planet. On a first date, they'll ask you about your dreams, your childhood wounds, and your thoughts on the global water crisis, sometimes all before the appetizer arrives. They might show up to the date with flowers… and an extra bouquet for your neighbor, just because she "looked sad last week."

Expect grand romantic gestures that double as activism. They're the type to take you to a candlelit dinner, only to reveal it's a fundraiser for displaced otters. 9s want to connect, deeply, soulfully, maybe even telepathically if you're open to it. They're excellent listeners, generous with their time and affection, and will probably end up helping your mom fix her Wi-Fi.

Boundaries? 9 women (and some men, but it takes longer), can lose themselves in love, like full identity-merge, "Your happiness is my happiness and also my emotional responsibility" levels of devotion. If you blink, they may have already planned your future together… and your children's community service schedules. Well, to be honest, even if you don't blink. 9s always have the future in mind. Their own, their own with yours, their own with yours and others.

Their idealism can also be a double-edged sword; they don't just want a partner; they want a soulmate who recycles and ideally reads minds.

## Dating Style of a 9: Masculine Edition

Dating a 9 man is like dating the lead singer of a soul band who also volunteers at animal shelters on the weekend. He's magnetic, deeply compassionate, and always seems to have a meaningful cause in his back pocket. He'll remember your birthday, your rescue dog's adoption day, and the time you casually mentioned wanting to see the Northern Lights, because that's where he'll suggest vacationing.

A 9 man loves deeply but can sometimes forget himself in the process. He'll happily help you move, listen to your existential crises, and encourage your dreams, often while quietly ignoring that he hasn't slept in three days. His heart is huge, his patience admirable, and yes, he might cry at commercials (don't tease him, he's fine with it, you need to be too).

He flirts with kindness, connection, and big-picture talk. Instead of "Wanna grab a drink?" you'll hear, "Do you ever wonder if we were meant to meet in this lifetime?" He wants love to feel meaningful, not just fun, so if you're looking for a partner who sees you (and occasionally your soul's purpose), this is your guy.

The shadow? He can get stuck in martyr mode or expect sainthood-level behavior from others ("Wait, you don't want to adopt three foster kittens today?"). But when balanced, a 9 man offers a rare mix of wisdom, loyalty, and a sense of humor about life's chaos, making him both inspiring and surprisingly fun to love.

## When They're Flirting:

The 9 flirt style is equal parts soulful gaze, heartfelt compliment, and accidental therapy session. Whether male or female, they don't do shallow, they want to connect deeply, even if it's over coffee and a croissant. Their flirting style often feels like they're auditioning for "Most Compassionate Human Alive," but somehow, it works.

They flirt by seeing you. Like, really seeing you. Expect intense eye contact, thoughtful questions about your childhood dreams, and compliments that hit deeper than "you look nice tonight." More like: "You light up when you talk about your art. That's rare. Don't ever stop." Their humor is self-deprecating and soft and will make you laugh without trying to "perform."

They show they're interested by making you feel safe. Expect warmth, calming energy, and subtle touches, a hand on your arm, a smile that says, "I get you." They notice you by offering compliments that feel personal: "The way you explained that just made so much sense." Their flirt is quiet but powerful: a mix of

*Debra Zachau*

soulful vulnerability and "I will feed you soup and also help you find your life purpose."

**The Darker Side of the 9 in Love**

After years of reading for countless 9s, I've noticed a pattern: their love runs deep, but so can their drama. A 9 doesn't just love you, they love you the way they want to be loved. Now, many Life Path numbers have this in their romantic repertoire, but if you don't mirror back a 9's efforts of love, well, brace yourself for the world's most delicate, slow-burning soap opera.

**Here's how it will likely unfold:**

First, they start quietly overanalyzing. You took longer than usual to text back, clearly something is wrong. They won't ask you directly (not yet). Instead, they'll run scenarios in their mind like a crime show detective piecing together clues from your emoji choices.

Next come the hints. A subtle sigh here. A vague, "No, I'm fine," there. If that doesn't work, they'll gather opinions: friends, coworkers, maybe even their therapist, to determine if your behavior is indeed as outrageous as it feels. Meanwhile, they're quietly skipping meals, hoping you'll notice their tragic aura and ask what's wrong... and then ask again... and maybe push them to really talk about it.

If the wound goes unacknowledged long enough? Enter passive-aggressive mode. The smiles get tighter, the silence gets heavier, and somewhere in the background, dramatic violins start playing. Weeks may pass. And then, one day, boom. Tears, chaos, and a dramatic airing of grievances you didn't know existed.

I know I'm being really tough on our beautiful 9s, and yes, we all struggle with the very same thing. But the reason I highlight our beautiful, wise souls of numerology is because of the time it will take a 9 to come to wise decisions. They will stay too long in jobs, relationships, and friendships, giving chance after chance. I love the idealistic halo they look through, seeing only the best in others until they can't anymore. Where others reassess, plan, and then act in a relatively short amount of time, 9s will stay. One reason is that they want to know, *really know*, they have been understood (spoiler: it's never satisfying enough). The second reason is that in the beginning, they painted a picture on their heart of how the relationship could go, then forgot it wasn't set in stone. Feelings change, and interests change.

The good news? Once a 9 learns to communicate upfront, they're some of the most forgiving, big-hearted partners out there. The very thing that can bring big trouble to a 9s peace can vibe in your favor! A 9 partner will give you room to stumble while learning how to grow a healthy, progressive relationship. Until then... keep snacks and tissues nearby.

**So a 9 has stolen your heart.**

**DO:**

**Do show appreciation often.** 9s give a lot, acknowledging their efforts makes them feel valued instead of taken for granted.

**Do ask how they're feeling.** Twice. The first "I'm fine" isn't always true; the second time, they'll tell you what's really going on.

**Do be patient with their process.** They're deep thinkers and need time to sort out their emotions before talking.

**Do match their kindness.** A 9 thrives in relationships where love is mutual, not one-sided.

**Do respect their ideals.** Even if you don't share them, acknowledging what they care about builds trust.

**DON'T:**

**Don't ignore subtle cues.** If their energy shifts, they've noticed something, and they're waiting for you to notice too.

**Don't mistake their forgiveness for forgetfulness.** They'll let things slide, but they do remember (and file it away for later processing). Remember, they are the legacy builders, the good and the bad.

**Don't dismiss their causes.** Whether it's saving animals or recycling properly, mocking their passions will cut deep.

**Don't push them to "get over it" quickly.** Their emotions are big; rushing them only makes the volcano blow sooner.

**Don't confuse their depth for drama.** They're not trying to be difficult; they're just wired to feel everything.

**Affirmations when Dating a 9**

"Their depth is not drama, it's devotion."

"I can appreciate their compassion without needing to fix everything for them."

"I give love freely, not just because they do."

"I understand their silences and trust them to share when they're ready."

"I respect their need to help others without feeling threatened by it."

"Their big feelings are part of their big heart."

"I celebrate their ideals even if I don't share all of them."

"I create space for them to process without taking it personally."

"I can love them as they are, not just as they are for me."

"Together, our love is compassionate, patient, and deeply meaningful."

## Their Spiritual Lessons:

Let go. Let go of the need to fix everyone. Let go of perfectionism in your purpose. Let go of that ex who still owes you $200 and a sincere apology. 9s must learn to help without losing themselves, forgive without over-sacrificing, and lead without judging those who haven't found their path yet (or are still wandering aimlessly in yoga pants).

They're here to give, yes, but also to live. To balance their heart with healthy boundaries, their vision with reality, and their emotional depth with just enough sarcasm to survive a holiday dinner.

The 9 is the walking embodiment of "namaste," but with a dash of messy idealism and a suitcase full of everyone else's problems. Approach gently. Accept the unsolicited advice. And prepare to leave the conversation feeling like you should volunteer more often and call your mom. They are old souls with bleeding hearts and brilliant minds. They're artists, mystics, volunteers, and spiritual CEOs. They see beauty in broken things and hope in hopeless places. But they also need to remember that saving the world is a team sport, and sometimes, it's okay to take a nap, let someone else hold the clipboard, and just be a human... instead of a full-time angel in sneakers.

**From a Life Path 9s perspective. Their perfect partner:**

Great Match. Easy flow, natural understanding; 8, 9, 33, and 44.

Good Match. Supportive, friendly, promising; 2, 4, 6, and 22.

Ambitious Match. Full of potential but needs work; 1, 7, and 11.

A Neutral Match. Could go either way, depends on maturity; 3, and 5.

# PART TWO

# Introduction to the Wild Ride of Master Numbers

The emotional extremes between the joy of a Christmas morning and a late-night DUI is the space in which Masters dance. They don't just step lightly through life; they twirl, stumble, fall dramatically, then leap back up with fireworks in their eyes. These are the souls who signed up for the deluxe karmic package: bigger hopes, bigger dreams, bigger meltdowns, and a relentless sense that they're "supposed" to do something huge with their time on Earth. No pressure, right? Except… everyone feels the pressure. Strangers sense it. Pets sense it. You probably sense it just reading this right now.

Master Numbers are born with an annoying little nudge from the Universe, a spiritual whisper that says, "You could move the world forward. Or backward. Totally up to you." And somewhere deep in their pre-birth soul briefing, they nodded like, "Sure, I got this," completely forgetting how chaotic Earth actually is. Newsflash: This planet is still the most chaotic reality show in the multiverse.

The thing about Master Numbers is that they know. They know at a soul level that they're here to do more. They may not know what the "more" is, but the longing is there, buzzing like a fluorescent light that never turns off. It shows up early, too. Picture being nine years old, clutching your stuffed animal, and already stressing about what you're supposed to do with your entire life. That's a Master Number childhood in a nutshell. While other kids are busy debating who gets the last slice of pizza, Master Numbers are quietly worrying about whether they're on the right path to save humanity.

Part of this intensity comes from their soul's energetic blueprint. Every soul incarnates with a kind of vibrational membrane, an invisible netting woven with lessons learned in previous lifetimes and is used to navigate this lifetime. Most people arrive with a standard weave. Master Numbers? They come in with the deluxe weave, one stitched with neon thread that says, "Extra credit available." Their potential is crystal clear, at least in the soul's eyes. The problem is that childhood trauma, toxic relationships, poor choices, or those annoying soul agreements (that we forget to read the fine print on), can cloud the clarity fast. Living on the densest planet in the universe doesn't help, either. Chaos is practically in the water supply here.

Still, even with all the blocks and detours, Master Numbers can't shake the sense that they're meant for something bigger. People expect more from them. They expect more from themselves. And while that sounds exhausting, and often is, it also comes with perks. Opportunities for growth show up like clockwork. You know that old saying, "When one door closes, another opens"? That's built into a Master Number's contract. The trick is noticing the open door instead of obsessing over the one that slammed shut. Unfortunately, flexibility is not their strongest suit.

That's where this book comes in. Think of it as your unofficial survival guide. Whether you are a Master Number, love a Master Number, or simply have to work with one without losing your sanity, this book is here to help. I'll shine a light on what makes these souls tick, the brilliance, the breakdowns, the incredible potential, and the maddening quirks.

Across these chapters, we'll explore each Master Number individually: 11, 22, 33, 44, and yes, even the wild child 55. We'll dive into what makes them magical, what makes them impossible, and what you absolutely need to know if you plan to love, date, or even just survive them. You'll learn how to spot them "in the wild," what their dating style says about their soul lessons, how they flirt (spoiler: badly, but adorably), and the spiritual growth they came here to chase.

By the end of this ride, you'll understand why Master Numbers can feel like the most fascinating, frustrating, beautiful puzzle pieces on the planet. And if you're one of them? Maybe, just maybe, you'll finally stop feeling like you're doing it wrong and start realizing *you were built to do it differently.*

## The Master Numbers at a Glance

### 11: Enlightenment on Legs

The 11 is what happens when you mix spiritual enlightenment with a haunted house full of feelings. Intuitive, inspiring, and often overwhelmed by the static of human existence, 11s are here to illuminate the world, sometimes despite themselves. These are the emotional meteorologists of the planet: they feel the weather before it hits. But that same sensitivity can trap them in cycles of self-doubt, anxiety, and magical thinking. They dream big, question everything, cry at beer commercials, and glow when they finally realize they're not broken, they're just tuned to a higher frequency.

**Key to potential:** Ground your energy, stop apologizing for being intense, and let your light do the talking.

## 22: The Master Builder

If the 11 is a lighthouse, the 22 is the construction crew building bridges, cities, and entire blueprints for the future, all while managing three group chats and a Google Drive folder no one else understands. These brilliant minds are capable of translating big spiritual ideas into real-life structures that actually work. But here's the catch: they spend so much time thinking, planning, and organizing, they sometimes forget that real impact requires actual physical action.

Dear 22: Step away from the spreadsheets. The path to your greatness isn't just on your laptop. Go outside. Plant something. Build a thing. Hug someone.

**Key to potential:** Take your ideas off the whiteboard and into the world. Your soul craves motion, not just models.

## 33: The Cosmic Artist

Ah, the 33. Equal parts healer, diva, empath, and holy trouble. These are the soul doctors with paintbrushes, born to inspire, soothe, and occasionally destroy your ego with a smile. 33s come in with beauty and compassion dripping from their aura, but beware: their shadow side includes arrogance so high up it's got a view of the city. They know they're special, sometimes too well, and forget that true spiritual greatness comes from humility, not applause.

To the beloved 33s: grab your ego from the clouds, bring it down to earth, and remember that a real healer gets on the floor with the wounded, and doesn't just lecture from a throne.

**Key to potential:** Your magic lives in service, not superiority. Get messy. Be real. Create anyway.

### 44: The Sacred Architect

Part protector, part powerhouse, 44s were born to build the unshakeable, whether it's a home, a business, or a sanctuary for others to finally exhale in. They are natural system-makers with an eye for legacy and a deep loyalty to those they love. But oh, the stubbornness. Once a 44 locks onto a belief or plan, they become a sentient bulldozer with feelings. Their soul's evolution depends on learning how to walk in someone else's shoes, even if those shoes are wildly impractical or don't match their aesthetic.

44s: You'll reach your power not just by building structures, but by understanding souls. Stretch your empathy until it snaps, then stretch it more.

**Key to potential:** Listen harder. Understand deeper. Your purpose is not just to build strong things, it's to build strong people.

### 55: The Disruptor

And now we meet the rebel philosopher: the 55. They're here to challenge everything: old systems, outdated traditions, and your patience. 55s are the ones pushing the planet forward by asking,

"But what if everything could be better?" They are chaos-bringers in the best sense, smashing through stagnation and blowing air into stuck places. When they see someone quitting, they push them forward. When they spot injustice, they push it back. When they sense arrogance, they swat it with glee.

Of course, all this disruption comes with a side of cynicism. These are the soul skeptics, the ones who've peeked behind every curtain and still aren't impressed. But don't let that fool you. Their heart is huge. Their courage? Unmatched.

**Key to potential:** Instead of just pushing against what's wrong, lean into building what's right. Disrupt, then rebuild with purpose.

In Summary...

The 11s drama and victimhood, the 22s inertia, the 33s sky-high ego, and the 44s steel-plated stubbornness... none of it holds a candle to the inner turbulence of the 55. But that's the whole point. Master Numbers didn't come to Earth to color inside the lines. They came to redraw the map. They are spiritual heavyweights in a world of cotton candy lessons. And whether they succeed wildly or flame out spectacularly, the truth is this: the world changes when Master Numbers show up.

And if you're one of them?

Don't worry. I wrote this book for you.

# The Hidden Numbers Beneath the Masters

Every Master Number holds another number within it; it's the smaller digit that's a part of the equation. And like a Russian nesting doll with unresolved childhood issues, that "inner number" never disappears. It whispers. It tugs. It shows up when the Master Number is tired, insecure, or spiraling in the Costco parking lot.

The smaller number is the foundation. The root. The hidden script playing beneath the spiritual high-definition broadcast. And let's be honest: Master Numbers don't rise to their full potential without first surviving the quirks and pitfalls of their inner number.

### Inside the 11: The Lonely 2

Buried inside every 11 is the energy of a Life Path 2, a soul who came here to learn relationships, cooperation, patience, diplomacy, and emotional connection.

So, naturally, 11s... would really just rather be left alone.

The irony here is cosmic comedy. The 11 needs solitude like plants need sun, they're hyper-sensitive, high-frequency, and often exhausted by the chaos of human interaction. But the 2 within them cry out for connection. For shared energy. For true partnership. It's as if their soul signed up for the "Advanced Enlightenment" course and forgot it was group work.

To grow, the 11 must learn to manage the pull: to honor the need for alone time without avoiding intimacy. Their spiritual homework is to make peace with humanity, one awkward brunch and Thanksgiving dinner at a time.

## Inside the 22: The Wounded 4

At the heart of every 22 is a solid, earthy 4, the number of security, systems, routines, and practical achievement. The 4 needs to feel safe, mentally, physically, and emotionally. But here's the twist: while the 4 may feel secretly unsafe and quietly yearn for inner stability, the 22 gets asked to broadcast that stability to the world.

That means vulnerability. Public vulnerability.

For a 4? That's a horror movie.

For a 22? It's a spiritual test.

The 22's greatness lies in creating sustainable systems that uplift others, but they can't do it while pretending they've got it all together. To fulfill their calling, they must learn to ask for help, admit they're struggling, and let others into the fortress. Only then does the 4 become the foundation for something truly transcendent.

## Inside the 33: The Flawless 6

The 33 holds the energy of the 6, the nurturing, caregiving, family-obsessed Life Path that needs things to be beautiful, functional, and deeply meaningful. But when distorted, the 6 becomes a perfectionist. Not just "neat and tidy" but "I-will-scrub-my-soul-before-you-see-it" levels of artificial grace.

For the 33, this becomes spiritual performance art. If a 33 can't be perfect, they need to fake it. Their shadow insists on a curated image of joy, healing, and light, even as it silently melts down in a locked bathroom.

True 33 power comes from dropping the mask. The world doesn't need your perfection. It needs your raw, messy, wildly honest compassion, the kind that raises their hand and says, "Me too," not "Look at how well I'm handling everything."

## Inside the 44: The Silent 8

The core of a 44 is the 8, the powerful, strategic, no-nonsense archetype of leadership, money, legacy, and fierce independence. But when the 8 is wounded, it doesn't shout. It simmers. The 44 channels this with terrifying precision. They may never raise their voice, but their belief in being "right" is as immovable as a glacier with a grudge. This isn't ego yelling at a dinner party. It's a rage they can't seem to shake.

What 44s must realize is that real strength isn't about quiet domination. It's about humility, dialogue, and genuine collaboration. The 8 inside them needs to evolve into empowerment, not control. When the 44 lets others in, the Master Manifestor becomes a Master Transformer.

## Inside the 55: The Untamed One

Here's where things get extra spicy. The 55 reduces to a 1, the Life Path of independence, innovation, and blazing your own trail. But unlike other Master Numbers, the 55 doesn't just contain the 1. It explodes it.

The 1 wants to lead. The 55 wants to burn it all down and rebuild in a new language. They are the first to do it a different way, no matter what "it" is. They don't follow rules; they question their existence. If a 55 enters a system, that system will never be the same.

But this untamed energy comes with no roadmap. There's no "safe" version of a 55 life. There's only courage, choice, and the deep soul-truth that if they don't live authentically, they'll feel caged in their own life.

Where the 1 says, "I lead," the 55 replies, "I reinvent."

Master Numbers carry high voltage. But it's their lower number roots that provide the grounding wire, the place where true lessons begin. Until they heal the shadows of their inner number, the "Master" part won't feel like a blessing. It'll feel like a burden. But once they integrate the wisdom of both? That's when the lightning hits the ground, and miracles happen.

# 11

# Life Path 11/2: The Intuitive Mystic With A Perfectionism Problem

We're officially stepping into the mysterious, magical, and mildly moody world of the 11. Oh, hello, chosen one.

If you're an 11, you've probably always suspected you were here for something more. More meaning. More depth. More late-night existential crises with herbal tea and a playlist titled "Songs to cry to while channeling spirit." A Master Number by design, 11s often walk around with a high-frequency antenna on their heads, picking up things most people miss, like someone's secret sadness or a ghost in the hotel lobby. (You're not crazy. You're just psychic. Really psychic.)

This path is blessed with intuitive knowing, visionary insight, deep empathy, and creativity that makes other people say, "Wait... how did you come up with that?" Whether it's art, counseling, writing, spiritual healing, or teaching the mystic arts, 11s are drawn to roles where they can channel wisdom and lift others. And their inner world? Oh, it's rich. So rich that sometimes they forget they're also expected to file taxes and eat lunch.

But, and there's always a "but" when perfection is on the menu, this brilliance comes with a cost. 11s tend to overthink, overfeel, and overextend themselves in ways that leave them teetering between enlightenment and emotional burnout. Their expectations (for themselves and others) can hover somewhere between "saintly" and "unattainable," and their tendency to withdraw, ghost, or spiral into anxious self-doubt is the stuff of spiritual sitcoms.

They want to save the world but forget they can't pour from an empty (chakra-infused) cup. They crave deep connection but sometimes isolate because nobody "gets" them. And don't even get them started on decision-making, because with their ability to see all the options (and then a few more), choosing anything can feel like Sophie's Choice meets a metaphysical migraine.

In short, being an 11 is like being born with a divine Wi-Fi signal and no user manual. It's both a blessing and a long, weird, enlightening journey, but one that's undeniably beautiful when embraced with humor, balance, and a few deep breaths.

When they were young, 11s are like tiny sages disguised in oversized backpacks. Sensitive, dreamy, and often deep beyond their years, these kids ask questions like "Why do people lie?" or "Do stars feel lonely?", usually right before bedtime, just to mess with your sleep. They can be shy and introspective one moment, then passionately defend a hurt classmate the next. Often misunderstood, they pick up on emotional undercurrents that adults miss entirely. You might find them sketching angels, writing poems, or talking to invisible forces with unnerving fluency. They don't always fit in, and heaven please help the ones who feel the need to. They were born *not* to try and fit in, but that's a tall order for any young person, let alone a young 11. They cry during animal rescue commercials, sense tension before it walks in the room, and have very specific opinions about the moon.

The grown-up 11 is an emotional tuning fork walking around in human form. Intuitive, spiritual, and often a little overwhelmed by the sheer depth of life, they live with one foot in this world and one foot in the Great Beyond (or at least a wellness retreat in Sedona). They are visionary thinkers and soulful creators, drawn to healing, helping, and sometimes hiding when it all gets too loud.

You'll recognize them at parties as: The ones who are either giving intuitive advice in the corner or sneaking out early because the vibes were off.

**Knowing, Loving, or Working with an 11**

When they channel their inner vision into something they believe in, history gets made. They become the teacher, the performer, the activist, the strategist, the one who doesn't just dream, but executes. They feel things deeply, yes, but they act with precision. Think of John Glenn, Kobe Bryant, Barack and Michelle Obama, Jennifer Lopez, all elevens who walk with conviction, discipline, and undeniable presence, while focused on "the other".

They see you.

And not in the "oh, you got a haircut" way. In the "I just noticed your soul is carrying grief from age six, and also your left shoulder is storing fear" kind of way.

11s are intuitive in a way that feels psychic, poetic, and a little unnerving. They can make you feel utterly exposed and completely cherished in the same sentence. If they love you, they will believe in you harder than you've ever believed in yourself. They will tell you your dreams matter and mean it. They can turn a dull Tuesday night into a deep conversation. They're visionaries, often ahead of their time. Give them space to explore their ideas, and they'll gift you with innovations, insights, and new ways to approach life. If you're working with an 11, they may not always hit deadlines, but when they do produce something, it's magic. Ethereal, original, and often far more profound than the assignment called for.

They are emotional empaths. They feel everything, your pain, your joy, your confusion, and they care deeply. Not performatively. Not because it looks good. They genuinely want to understand your inner world and help heal it, even if it overwhelms them in the process. They are also incredibly inspiring. Their mere presence makes you want to be a better version of yourself, more honest, more compassionate, more alive. You won't know whether to thank them or panic about the level of self-work you suddenly feel compelled to do.

Look, being close to an 11 is like living next door to a moonbeam with Wi-Fi issues. Sometimes they're fully lit up and downloading universal insight like they're wired into the Divine... and sometimes they just kind of... go offline. It's not personal. They need more quiet time than most. Sometimes, they just need to unplug and stare into space for a few hours. Or a weekend. Or a lunar cycle.

Whether it's love, friendship, or something soul-adjacent, an 11 seeks connection that feels meaningful, intuitive, and growth-oriented. They want depth, not surface. Substance, not small talk. A person who can hold space for their complex inner world without trying to fix or define it.

They may cry at refrigerator magnet poetry. Or just because you asked them, "How's your day going?" and the question felt so sincere. Loyalty is non-negotiable. Authenticity is everything. They're less interested in "perfect" and more drawn to people who are genuine, self-aware, and curious about life. And while they may seem emotionally complex, their core need is simple: to feel safe being their whole self, intuitive, intense, idealistic, and all.

When it comes to communication, 11s are fluent. But unfortunately, Earth mostly runs on logistics and calendar invites. They may forget your birthday dinner, miss a deadline, or disappear mid-conversation, not because they don't care, but because their mind got pulled away by a thought about the topic, and they are trying not to interrupt.

Relationships? 11s dream of deep, epic, transcendent love... as long as it doesn't involve too much small talk, expectations, or long hours of togetherness that could interfere with their nightly routine. They crave connection but need solitude like oxygen. They want a divine union. A soulmate. Someone who gets them without words. But they also need long periods alone to recharge, which may feel like abandonment to anyone who hasn't caught onto their brilliant quirks.

Also, yes, they can occasionally slip into spiritual martyr mode. "Why is the world so heavy?" they'll whisper, arms dramatically outstretched, when confronted with a minor inconvenience. But even their most melodramatic moments are usually sincere; they're just trying to find the divine pattern in every bump, bruise, or missed text message.

At work, 11s may not always take the straightest path to the finish line. But when they do show up with a finished product? It's not just good; it's inspired. Their ideas are often ahead of their time. Just don't ask them to write it all down in bullet points. That would hurt their soul. They need more words to make it clear.

The 11's shadow side isn't "flaky." It's more like being preoccupied with the beauty of the galaxy. They're juggling dimensions in their mind while trying to remember where they put their phone. Yes, they can be emotionally high-maintenance, spiritually distracted, and sometimes a bit dramatic, but they also bring more depth, beauty, and meaning to your life than ten regular humans standing in a row with matching designer shoes.

They might not always show up on time, but when they do? They'll remind you why you believed in love, art, and humanity in the first place.

## How to Spot an 11 in the Wild

You're at a party. Someone walks in wearing something that looks like it was ethically sourced from the dreams of a visionary. They lock eyes with the houseplant. Not you. The plant. They pause. Their head tilts slightly, as if listening to a message you can't hear. Congratulations. You may have just spotted an 11.

Identifying them in their natural habitat isn't difficult once you know the signs. They emit a subtle glow of "something deeper going on here," even when they're just ordering coffee. It's in the eyes, soulful, wide, and a little haunted. Like they just saw the meaning of life and want to commit it to memory before they forget.

Here are your first clues:

**The aura**: There's a hum around them. It's not visible, but you feel it. They radiate a mix of high-frequency wisdom and mild panic, like a monk who just discovered they double-booked a silent retreat and a dental appointment. They're magnetic. People tell them secrets in elevators. Strangers feel oddly comforted by their presence, but also vaguely guilty about their level of self-care.

**The conversation style**: If you're trying to make small talk, bless you. 11s don't really do surface-level conversations. You'll mention the weather, and suddenly you're in a three-hour heart-share about universal love, quantum alignment, and a recurring dream about a fox in a library, and you love the time spent.

**The wardrobe:** Their outfit might be a little… otherworldly. Think: soft fabrics, flowing silhouettes, or something with moons on it. They like clothing that breathes, sways, and has a "don't try to define me" energy. Bonus points if they have a notebook with stars on the cover.

**The eyes (again):** Truly, it's worth repeating. 11s have those eyes. You know the ones. Deep. Watery. Wide. Like they just had a conversation with their higher self in the produce aisle. You will feel seen, known, and maybe slightly judged by your own ancestors.

**Their energy field:** When grounded, they are peaceful, radiant, and wise. When not grounded (which may be often), they're glitchy, disoriented, and weirdly obsessed with signs. Like, "The car in front of me had 222 on the plate. That means I'm supposed to go to Bali." They're constantly seeking synchronicity like it's oxygen.

At work in public places, you'll find them quietly creating beauty, facilitating healing, or softly disassociating at their desk while processing the emotional trauma of everyone in the building. They may be artists, therapists, spiritual teachers, indie musicians, or energy consultants, whose job you still don't fully understand, but you can't get in because their calendars are packed. They're the one who volunteers for a compassion project, write a ten-page email about the soul of the team, then disappear for three days to "reset" their energy.

**Their technology use:** 11s have a strange relationship with tech. They adore it (all those rabbit holes!), but it constantly short-circuits around them. Phones freeze. Apps crash. Wi-Fi disappears mysteriously when they're trying to send a heartfelt message. You can blame it on Mercury retrograde, but it's more of a lifestyle.

**Bonus identification trick:** Say something flippant about astrology, numerology, or the Law of Attraction. An 11 will flinch.

Not outwardly. Just... subtly. Like a psychic papercut. Then, with unnerving calm, they'll offer a gentle, poetic correction, and somehow make you feel like the conversation just got blessed by a choir of invisible angels.

11s are dreamy, complex, beautiful enigmas who walk through life like tuning forks in a drum circle. They are part mystic, part anxious raccoon, and part divine reminder that we are all made of stars... with unresolved emotional baggage. Once you learn to spot them, you'll never unsee them. And honestly? Your life will be better for it.

## The Dating Style of an 11

Soulmate or soul storm? ...Yes...

Dating them is not so much a romantic experience as it is a sacred initiation. You don't just swipe right on an 11, you enter a vortex. One moment you're flirting over tacos, the next you're locked in a conversation about whether time is linear and if you've met before in another lifetime. You probably have.

They're drawn to partners who radiate purpose, someone with spiritual curiosity, creative passions, and the emotional stamina to go deep without running for cover. Dating is casual, for the longest time, until it isn't. Then, we're talking about an energetic merging of two luminous beings who may or may not start a podcast together.

But make no mistake, under that soft-spoken mystic vibe is a mind that can slice through BS like a samurai. 11s are emotionally intelligent, perceptive, and often psychic in relationships, which is great until you realize they already suspect a secret you never intended to share.

With all that insight comes sensitivity. 11s can be emotionally porous, soaking up their partner's mood like a sponge in a thunderstorm. They don't need a savior or a fixer, they need someone calm, grounded, and strong enough to let them be complex without trying to make them "easier." Give them space for their dreams, a soft place to land when the world gets noisy, and someone who believes, not just in them, but in something bigger.

At first, they're alluring. Mysterious. Deep. A little hard to read, like a poem scrawled in the margins of an ancient book about soul contracts. You'll feel drawn in, magnetized by something in their energy field, even if you've never heard of an energy field. They'll likely make you feel special. Not because they're trying to, but because they see things in you no one else does. They'll reflect back your potential, your pain, your hidden dreams, like a human mirror covered in sparkles and fog.

They'll likely share their dreams with you early on, literal dreams, often full of symbols, ancestors, and haunted barns. They'll talk about intuition, déjà vu, and synchronicities. If you roll your eyes, they'll notice and vanish. But if you lean in? Buckle up. You're now on a totally different, mind-blowing train, no stops, no refunds. Expect conversations that feel like therapy, prayer, and psychedelic journeying all rolled into one. Also, expect sudden silence. If you take their vanishing personally, the relationship won't last. They're not ghosting, they're recalibrating, so the time between you when you are together is perfect.

The challenge with dating an 11 isn't love, it's staying grounded. Their feelings are real, but they fluctuate like the tides during a full moon eclipse in Pisces. If they're struggling, they may idealize you, then feel betrayed the moment you act like a mortal. Their expectations are sky-high, but their own sense of self-worth often lags behind, causing them to question everything. (Including whether you really meant it when you said you loved them, or if you're just saying it out of Karmic obligation.) Emotional storms are possible. Sometimes frequent. But here's the trick: if you can stay calm while they ride it out, they'll see you as their anchor, their person. They may never say it that plainly, but they'll know. And they'll stay.

## Dating an 11: Masculine Edition

So, you've fallen in love? Congrats.

The 11 man is a walking paradox. He wants intimacy, but disappears. He says he doesn't believe in labels, but then gives you the newest top of the line tech gadget no one else can find, let alone buy. He'll ask you how you really feel about the concept of past lives, and then kiss you like he's found you in every single one.

This is not your average guy. This will be your emotionally mysterious philosopher. He's half love song, half question mark. He feels deeply but doesn't always overtly show it because he needs to assess whether you're ready for the explanation. So, he stares at you a little too long. Or writes you a song. Or sends you an article about the energetic weight of collective grief.

Don't expect a chase, expect a mood. Masculine 11s don't pursue in the traditional "let's grab drinks" kind of way. They orbit. They observe. They vibe. They're the ones sitting quietly at a party, reading your energy while pretending to look at their phone. You'll know they're interested if they lean in slightly when you talk... then surprised when they vanish in the crowd for the rest of the party, only to race to the door to help you on with your coat when getting up to leave. Yeah, that kinda guy. Heaven help him if you get solid proof that he likes you. I really don't know why they're this way, but it's been my experience that most are.

Once you're both openly on the same page and call it a relationship, all this tomfoolery stops, which makes the confusion worthwhile. When they do express interest, it often comes in the form of emotionally intense glimmers. A look that lingers a little too long. A message that reads like it should be carved into stone tablets. A casual, "I dreamed of you last night," followed by... no context.

You'll spend the first phase of the relationship wondering, "Is this something? Am I imagining this?" And that's when you know... yes, you are officially dating an  11 man.

As mentioned earlier, once in, they're all in. Emotionally? Yes. Spiritually? Deeply. Practically? Well, trying. He may text you beautiful, philosophical questions at 2 a.m., like, "Do you ever feel love is the key to all timelines?" And yet, he might forget that your date was tonight, not tomorrow. Not because he doesn't care. Because time, in his mind, is fluid and optional. (Yep, like our distracted 5).

They often have trouble with vulnerability, not because they're emotionally unavailable, but because they're emotionally oversaturated. He feels so much that he short-circuits. So, instead of sharing his feelings, he might go silent.

And yes, the victim energy with both male and female can occasionally sneak in. If they feel misunderstood, they may spiral. Not with anger, but with wounded silence, heavy sighs, or moody playlists about betrayal. The good news? When given time, they'll come back. The bad news? They might ask you what you learned during the emotional absence.

When grounded and connected, 11s are lovers of the highest caliber. Intense. Present. Devotional. And affection becomes a ceremony.

But when they're ungrounded? They can drift. Disconnect. Retreat into overthinking. You may catch them staring off mid-cuddle, lost in a memory of a dream that might have been a prophecy. Don't take it personally. Just gently guide them back to Earth. Snacks always work…just sayin'.

## If you're all in with an 11…

**DO:**

**Do hold space.** They process slowly and feel quickly. If you can just be still while they sort out what's theirs vs. what's the emotional atmosphere of the tri-city area. And love you forever if you give them room for this process.

**Do give them space.** Counterintuitive? Yes. But vital. Alone time isn't a rejection, it's soul maintenance. Their inner world is full of downloads, metaphors, energy shifts, and intuitive nudges. Let them reboot. They'll come back with a clearer heart and possibly a poem.

**Do be emotionally honest.** They can read energy like it's printed in bold. Say what you mean. Mean what you say. Don't smile while stewing inside. It throws off their radar and makes them suspicious.

**Do encourage their dreams.** Even the weird ones. Especially the weird ones. They may not always finish what they start, but feeling supported in the vision gives them wings, even if they never build the nest.

**Do keep your own spiritual center.** They're not here to carry your healing. They'll try, but it will burn them out and create an imbalance. Do your own work. Show them you're a well-rounded person, not a project.

**DON'T:**

**Don't dismiss their intuition.** If they say something "feels off," don't mock it. They probably picked up on something real. They've been reading vibes since before preschool.

**Don't try to keep it surface-level.** "Chill" dating doesn't work here. If you're just looking for a plus-one for brunch and beach selfies, keep scrolling. They're not trying to fill your photo album. They're here to open your soul.

**Don't take their need for solitude personally.** I'll say it again: Alone time is sacred. Let them float back to Source, and they'll return with eyes full of stars (and maybe a tarot card tucked into their shoe).

**Don't expect consistency in human time.** They live in soul time. Appointments and schedules may occasionally fall victim to spiritual fatigue, sudden dreams, or a passing cloud that reminded them of a karmic wound.

**Don't push for logic when they're in a feeling state.** Trying to "reason" with an 11 mid-meltdown is like trying to teach a dolphin algebra. Or ask them to "be more normal." (That ship sailed three lifetimes ago.) It's not the moment. Offer presence, not problem-solving.

## Emergency Affirmations when Loving an 11

"I trust their silence isn't distance, it's depth."

"I don't need to understand everything to love fully."

"We are learning each other's language, even if theirs is mostly metaphors."

"I am grounded. They are floating. Together, we defy gravity."

*I know, I know that line is so sappy! Sometimes my writing guides get like, really deep Rumi vibes. (It's my 11 showing). But ya gotta admit, it would make a great greeting card...or tee shirt... (You're welcome.) Tip of the hat to Aley Martin, whose Rumi video inspired my writing today.*

"They don't need to be healed, they need to feel safe."

"I understand their need for solitude isn't rejection. It's soul maintenance."

## Spiritual Lessons of an 11

Why did they sign up for this lifetime in the first place (besides the thrilling opportunity to overthink everything)?

11's are here to learn that their sensitivity isn't a weakness, it's a gift. That intuition isn't something to hide, it's a compass. That feeling everything doesn't mean breaking under the weight, it means becoming wise enough to carry *only what's theirs*.

They're also here to integrate both worlds, the spiritual and the human. To learn how to be in this life, not just observe it like an overwhelmed psychic tourist. They're here to connect, even when it's hard. To trust people, even when it's messy. To shine, even when they feel invisible.

They came to learn boundaries, discernment, and grounded service. Their enlightenment is real, but they're here to learn how to live it, not just vibe with it. They came to anchor light, not just absorb it.

## What Life Path 11 Came to Teach Us

They teach us that feelings are sacred. That intuition is intelligence. That hope is not naïve, it's holy. They remind us that pain is not the enemy, and beauty isn't always tidy.

Through their vulnerability, they show us how to be brave.

Through their chaos, they remind us we are more than our structure.

Through their love, they awaken parts of us we forgot were even there.

They came to whisper truths the world forgot how to hear.

To love without armor. To see without judgment. To feel without fear.

Being in a relationship with an 11 isn't easy, but it is worth it. They'll stretch you emotionally, spiritually, and sometimes physically (they love a nature hike to "reconnect with Source"). But if you're looking for a partner who sees your soul, speaks your language, and genuinely wants to evolve with you... This is your person.

**From a Life Path 11's perspective. Their perfect partner:**

Great Match. Easy flow, natural understanding; 1, 3, 8, and 11.

Good Match. Supportive, friendly, promising; 5, 6, 7, 9, and 33.

Ambitious Match. Full of potential but needs work; 2. 4, 22, and 44.

# Life Path 22/4: The Sacred Blueprint

They build. But also... they spiral. Then come back and build better.

If the 11 is enlightenment on legs, the 22 is God's project manager, clipboard in one hand, sacred purpose in the other. This is the Master Builder, the one who came here to take soul-level visions and drag them, lovingly and a little anxiously, into real-world form. Not just ideas, but structures. Systems. Programs. Legacies. Think healing centers, non-profits, eco-villages, conscious corporations, and apps that save the planet.

22s are rooted in the grounded, get-things-done energy of the 4, but with extra voltage. While the 4 builds solid walls, the 22 builds empires, or tries to, usually while drinking too much coffee and rewriting their mission statement at 2 a.m. They have both the vision and the stamina to change the world, but they often forget they're still human. This is the paradox of the 22: they're trying to channel divine blueprints through a body that still needs sleep, tacos, and the occasional soft breakdown in the car.

At their best, 22s are calm in a crisis, reliable to the bone, and deeply mission driven. They have a gift for turning chaos into order without losing the soul of the vision. They're not flashy. They're not loud. But they are the ones quietly holding the entire project, or family, or company, or relationship together, usually without getting much credit. They'll tell you they're "just helping," but somehow the entire thing would collapse if they weren't involved.

And yet, for all their brilliance, 22s live with an almost constant, low-key pressure to be more. There's always a next step. A better way. A more efficient system to build, a higher purpose to serve. This inner drive is powerful, and it's also exhausting. The moment they finish one big project, they're already wondering if it was "enough." And in their minds, it never quite is.

The shadow side isn't darkness, it's depletion. They push themselves too hard, too long, in too many directions. Rest feels lazy. Asking for help feels weak. Feelings are inconvenient. And perfection? It's the standard. If a project doesn't meet their internal blueprint of excellence, they may drop it entirely. Or worse, never start it at all. That business plan, podcast, social initiative, or dream house? It's sitting in a folder somewhere, just waiting for them to feel "ready."

Emotionally, 22s can be hard to read. They're practical and often reserved. Many learned early on that feelings get in the way of getting things done, so they compartmentalize. You'll know they're overwhelmed when they start snapping at printers or fixing the toaster at 3 a.m. Vulnerability isn't natural for them. It has to be earned. But once they let you in, you're part of their sacred circle, and they will go to the mat for you. They are loyal, protective, and generous to a fault, especially when they feel appreciated (spoiler: they rarely do, so don't stop saying it).

Their need for control can sneak in like a well-dressed guest at a party who slowly takes over the playlist, the snacks, and eventually the furniture layout. They don't mean to dominate; they just know how things should be done. And watching other people fumble through something they could fix in five minutes is genuinely painful for them. So, they step in. Quietly. Efficiently. And usually without telling you they rewrote your entire launch plan.

At their worst, they confuse busyness with worth and achievement with identity. But at their best? They remind us that dreams without structure are just folly. That purpose isn't something we talk about; it's something we build, step by step, with love and grit.

Now, if you've made it this far and you're thinking, "Wait a minute... my spouse, boss or roommate is a 22 and I have never seen them work hard on goals, color-code anything, or build a community garden," and, you're not wrong. This is where the mystery gets especially fun (and relatable).

You see, while the 22 has the soul blueprint of a high-functioning, legacy-level master builder, their day-to-day reality can look like complete and utter chaos. Not always, but often enough that I've seen a pattern. After doing thousands of sessions over the years, I can say with confidence: some of the most gifted 22s I've ever met have had the messiest offices, the most delayed email replies, and the highest ratio of unwashed mugs to actual furniture in their creative zones.

This is where relationships matter, especially with 22s. If you love one, live with one, or work alongside one, you need to understand that their external world doesn't always reflect the brilliance of what's going on inside. They can be building something profound in their mind while the kitchen catches fire. They'll miss birthdays, delete half their to-do list, and forget they own pants, but hand them a purpose, and they'll change the world with it.

Let me paint you a scene I've encountered more than once: You walk into your 22 partner's workspace and are hit with what can only be described as a visual poem of disarray. There's mustard spilled on a spoon, under a towel, which is somehow under the printed first draft of their ten-year project projection, you know, the one you're both working on. There are sticky notes, printouts, three pens that don't work, and the unmistakable hum of deep, focused genius... surrounded by clutter that looks like a chihuahua has been defending you from hidden danger, and with that, stirred things up a bit.

And here's the part that's equal parts funny and tragic: the moment you, with love, concern, or sheer horror, point this out, the 22 stares at the towel-mustard disaster as if they're seeing it for the very first time. Like it materialized just now, from another dimension. They'll blink slowly. Then, in an emotional panic spiral, you might hear:

"I think I might have ADHD."

"I'm probably on the spectrum."

"It's childhood trauma. My mom never labeled jars."

In other words, instead of just admitting, "Oh wow, yeah, that's a mess, I got really into something, and the room disappeared," they default to a full identity crisis.

But here's the truth: They were deeply involved with a cool thing. Their genius hijacked their frontal lobe, and they dropped into a zone of flow where time, mustard, and social expectations ceased to exist. And that's not a disorder. That's just... being a 22 on a mission.

## How to Spot a 22 in the Wild

Spotting a 22 in the wild can be tricky. They don't typically announce themselves with glitter or ego. Unlike the flamboyant 3 or the emotionally broadcasted 11, the 22 tends to fly under the radar. They're not flashy. They're not loud. But if you know what to look for, their presence is unmistakable, like a deep bass tone under a note that holds the whole thing together. Outwardly, they may look like every other adult carrying the weight of 47 responsibilities and a caffeine dependency. But lean in. Notice how they're holding the world together without anyone asking them to. That's your first clue.

**Confident Posture:** They stand like they've been called to greatness since birth, which, in fairness, they kind of have. Shoulders back, head held high, and an aura that suggests they've already solved three problems on the way to this conversation.

**Focused Eye Contact:** You will feel seen, and possibly, slightly audited. 22s lock eyes with intensity, not because they're intimidating, but because their brain is scanning your soul and planning a project timeline.

**Purposeful Movements:** They don't fidget. They glide. Every step has a mission; every turn has intention. Watching them move is like watching someone edit a spreadsheet in real life.

**Authoritative Tone:** Their voice says, "Trust me, I've thought this through," even if they're just ordering lunch. If they're managing a group, it's less "chaos" and more "high-performance team in action."

**Calm Body Language:** Even under pressure, they rarely show cracks. Their stillness is powerful, their presence grounding. If a building was on fire, you'd probably follow the 22, they'd already have the evacuation route mapped and a better building design in mind.

**Emotionally, they're measured.** Not cold but contained. When everyone else is panicking, the 22 is scanning for a plan B. Or rebuilding plan A. Or calmly reassembling a broken lamp while explaining tax benefits. They're the kind of person who comforts you during a crisis by reworking your budget, which is weirdly comforting.

**"Just fine thanks."** If you're close to them, you'll notice something else: they rarely complain. That doesn't mean they're fine. It just means they don't believe complaining fixes anything. They'll quietly suffer through impossible workloads, personal burnout, and inner emotional storms, and when you ask how they're doing, they'll probably say, "I'm okay," while scurrying off to the place they feel the safest, which is whatever project is on their screen.

They won't show off their spiritual side the way an 11 or 7 might. But if you talk long enough, they'll reveal a deep sense of service, a belief in long-term good, and an almost uncomfortable ability to connect mystical concepts to real-world logistics. They're the person who doesn't just "believe in manifestation," they've also built an app to track it.

And perhaps most telling of all: they carry a quiet heaviness, like someone who knows they're meant to do something important but haven't fully figured out how to pull it off without losing their mind. They feel pressure without a clear origin. Responsibility that no one assigned. And yet, they keep showing up.

They're not loud. Not obvious. But essential. The foundation beneath so many things that work, even if their space looks like a laundry-themed escape room.

## The Dating Style of a 22

When it comes to romance, a 22 doesn't just fall in love, they project-manage it. They aren't dating just to get out of the sun; they're dating with a purpose. You can expect an initial vetting process to resemble an invitation to present a spur-of-the-moment pitch deck for a new startup. But don't let that intimidate you, deep down, 22s are hopeless idealists disguised as grounded, goal setting, legend builders.

22 individuals are attracted to partners who get stuff done, bonus points if you own a planner and know how to use it. They swoon

for shared ambition, mutual purpose, and a solid vision for their future. (That's with or without a partner by the way.) Love languages include acts of service, long-term planning, with a dash of emotional avoidance.

Dating a 22 is like falling in love with the architect of a future that hasn't been built yet. You may not fully understand what's happening, but it feels important. Like you're being slowly folded into a blueprint you can't quite see, one they started sketching years before you arrived. On the surface, 22s are calm, collected, and capable. They don't come in hot with flowers and sonnets. They show up with a steady presence, a reasonable plan, and an offer to help hang your new shelving unit. Their affection may not be loud, but it is useful. If a 22 likes you, they will try to improve your life, whether you asked them to or not.

They're not into grand gestures for the sake of drama. They're into functional devotion. Need your taxes organized? Car repaired? Website launched? They're on it. Their version of flirting might look like quietly fixing your broken light fixture while asking thoughtful questions about your family.

But make no mistake, behind their practical exterior is a deeply romantic heart. The 22 craves partnership. They dream of building a life, a home, maybe a legacy, something that matters. They don't want to date just to pass the time. They want something real. Something stable. Something they can count on.

The catch? They'll rarely tell you that directly.

You see, 22s are used to being the stable one. The one people lean on. So, when it comes to love, they're often careful. Guarded. Even a little emotionally distant at first. Not because they don't feel, but because they feel a lot, and they don't want to unravel unless it's safe to do so. They want love that's earned, tested, and real. And until they're sure you're it? They'll play it cool.

Sometimes too cool.

They might downplay their feelings, act like they're "just seeing where it goes," or avoid vulnerability entirely by staying busy. If they start reorganizing their garage instead of answering your texts, don't panic. This is their love language. It's avoidance dipped in productivity. They're not ghosting. They're thinking things through with movement.

And once they're in? Oh, they're in. Deeply committed, fiercely loyal, and constantly looking for ways to make your shared life better. They're the partner who remembers the little things and thinks ahead. They want to protect you from every minor inconvenience the future could possibly hold. You won't always feel fireworks, but you'll feel safe. And eventually, that becomes a deeper kind of passion: one built on trust, endurance, and knowing you've got someone in your corner, no matter what.

That said, if a 22 hasn't done their emotional homework, intimacy can be... complicated. Vulnerability doesn't come naturally. They might intellectualize feelings, deflect affection, or dive headfirst into work every time emotions get real. Their deepest fear isn't rejection, it's inadequacy. So, if they feel like they can't live up to the kind of partner they should be, they might sabotage the connection before you have a chance to see them fumble.

And yes, their need for control can also creep into the relationship. They may want to tweak your schedule, adjust your habits, or gently nudge you toward "a better way" of doing things. But at the heart of that is this: they just want things to work. They want you to work. Not because you're broken, but because they believe in your potential and want to build something amazing with you.

## Dating a 22: Masculine Edition

Strong, steady, and possibly planning your entire future in Excel. Falling for this guy is like meeting a real-life action figure, not because they're swinging from ropes or wrestling bears (though they might surprise you), but because they seem solid. Reliable. Like someone who could both fix your leaky sink and negotiate your car payment in the same afternoon. This is the partner who doesn't just say they want stability, they are stability. Even when their desk looks like a craft store and a hardware aisle exploded, there's an underlying sense of order in how they move through life. They don't woo you with flashy speeches or over-the-top gestures. They win you over with presence, consistency, and the kind of competence that makes you feel like the house could catch fire and they'd calmly grab the extinguisher and your favorite sweater before you even smell smoke.

The challenge in dating a 22 isn't love. It's emotional access. They will show you their plans before they show you their wounds. They will give you structure before they give you softness. And unless they feel truly seen and safe, they may keep a part of themselves in reserve, locked behind a vault labeled "maybe later."

But under that "I've got this" exterior is a softer truth: they're not immune to vulnerability, they just package it differently. Instead of saying, "I'm scared we're moving too fast," they might ask if you're sure you're saving enough for retirement. Instead of telling you they miss you, they'll check if your tires are properly inflated. Their love language is acts of service dressed as logistics.

When courting you, they tend to observe more than pursue. They're not about rapid-fire texts and constant digital contact. Instead, they'll watch, listen, and assess if you're someone they can build with, and yes, I do mean build. If they don't see a shared future potential, they'll politely keep things casual. If they do? The subtle shift will be unmistakable. They'll start integrating you into their plans, inviting you into projects, and offering to help with things that seem minor but are actually their way of saying, "You matter to me".

Once they commit, their loyalty is intense. They want to protect you, provide for you, and partner with you in tangible ways. But here's the thing: he can get so focused on being the rock in the relationship that they forget rocks don't talk much. You might go weeks without hearing a deep emotional disclosure, not because they don't feel, but because they're expressing themselves through action rather than words. If you're waiting for flowery monologues, you may be waiting a long time. If you can see love in the freshly repaired shelf or the perfectly planned road trip, you'll feel it every day.

Their shadow in relationships often comes from the same place as their strength: responsibility. If they start feeling inadequate, financially, emotionally, or in their ability to "handle things," they may shut down or overcompensate by working longer hours, fixing non-essential problems, or withdrawing into projects. This isn't rejection, it's their way of regaining a sense of control before letting you back into the emotional space.

If you can meet them halfway, offering patience, clarity, and reassurance that you value them, not just what they do, you'll see the quiet transformation. 22s will open up in ways that feel rare, precious, and unshakably real. And once they feel safe, they're all in. They will guard your dreams, invest in your future, and stand beside you long after other people would have walked away.

Pro Tip for Loving a 22: If he's sanding a piece of wood, fixing a hinge, or fiddling with their laptop, that's the moment to talk about feelings. Something about keeping their hands busy helps their heart open.

## So a 22 has stolen your heart...

How to keep your Master Builder from quietly imploding.

**DO:**

**Do appreciate what they build, in every sense.** When a 22 invests in you, they're not just giving love; they're laying foundations. Whether they're helping you file your taxes, plotting out a business plan, or reorganizing your closet in a way that "just makes sense," see it for what it is: devotion in action. Compliment it. They'll beam.

**Do give them space to work... but remind them to rest.** A 22 can disappear into a project like it's a black hole. They don't always notice when their lunch turned into dinner or when "just one more thing" became 2 a.m. You can be the gentle hand pulling them out before burnout becomes their new address.

**Do speak their language: which is...results.** They respond to concrete feedback. "You make me feel safe" hits harder than "I love you", not because they don't want love, but because safety is love to them. Tell them exactly how their actions affect you in a positive way.

**Do encourage vulnerability without forcing it.** They have feelings. Deep ones. But sharing them may feel like walking on a high wire. Show them you can be trusted with their truth, and they'll eventually let you all the way in.

**Do stand beside them, not in front of them.** They want a partner, not a competitor. Collaboration lights them up. Power struggles shut them down.

**DON'T:**

**Don't mistake busy for distant.** If they seem absorbed in something, it's not because they've stopped caring. It's because they can't relax until the problem/project/plan is resolved. Let them finish their mental construction work, and they'll reappear.

**Don't criticize their methods mid-build.** You might have a better way, but 22s are meticulous. Interrupting their process feels like pulling the steering wheel while they're on the highway. Let them finish before you offer tweaks.

**Don't push them into emotional marathons when they're spent.** If they're physically and mentally tired, heavy talks will either bounce off or trigger shutdown mode. Pick your timing wisely, preferably after snacks and a little quiet.

**Don't treat their service as "just how they are."** If they're doing things for you, it's not autopilot, it's effort. Acknowledge it. Otherwise, they'll start to feel invisible, which for a 22 is the fast lane to resentment.

**Don't expect them to wing it.** They like plans, frameworks, and knowing the lay of the land. Last-minute chaos is *not* their love language.

## Emergency Affirmations when Loving a 22

Repeat these when they've been in their office for five hours, still "just finishing something," and you're debating whether to knock.

"Their focus is not rejection, it's commitment."

"They are building for us, not away from us."

"I can trust their process, even if it's slower than mine."

"They express love through action, and I see it clearly."

"I value who they are, not just what they produce."

## The Spiritual Lessons of a Life Path 22

The 22 came here with a cosmic contract that basically says: You're capable of building something lasting, something meaningful, something that changes lives. No pressure, right? This is a lifetime of turning vision into form, of taking what most people only dream about and anchoring it into the real world. The 22's spiritual lesson is that success isn't just about the size of what they build, but the heart inside it. They're here to learn that true legacy is measured in the lives touched, not the square footage covered.

A big part of this lesson is learning how to let people in. The 22 can be so self-reliant that asking for help feels like admitting weakness. But their growth hinges on collaboration, not isolation. They're here to learn that vulnerability doesn't weaken the foundation; it strengthens it. That perfection is the enemy of progress. And that you can't build a world worth living in if you burn yourself out before you get there.

They're also learning that stability doesn't have to be rigid. Flexibility is not failure; it's wisdom. The Universe will keep handing them opportunities to adapt until they realize the most beautiful structures are the ones that can bend without breaking.

The 22 came to learn how to balance responsibility with joy. Yes, they're here to build and contribute, but not at the cost of their own aliveness. They must learn that rest is not laziness, and that their worth isn't measured solely by output. They're here to learn that the heart of leadership isn't control, it's trust. Trusting their own vision, trusting the people they collaborate with, and trusting that they don't have to carry the entire blueprint alone. And most importantly, they came to learn that they are human first, Master Builder second. They are allowed to be messy. They are allowed to be unsure. They are allowed to put the hammer down and just sit in the sun for an afternoon without the sky falling.

## What They Came Here to Teach

22s are here to show the rest of us that big dreams don't have to stay in the clouds. They teach by example, by showing that structure and spirit can live in the same house, and that sacred work is built one practical step at a time. They teach us that real change is not made in dramatic bursts, but through steady, thoughtful effort. They teach that service to others can be both grounded and visionary. And perhaps most beautifully, they remind us that purpose is not about chasing perfection, it's about building something that matters and letting it be alive, flexible, and human.

Through their quiet dedication, they show that legacies are built in conversations, choices, and moments that may seem small but accumulate into something extraordinary. They're living proof that you don't need to shout to make an impact; sometimes, you just need to show up, again and again, until the work is done.

Dating, befriending, or working with a 22 is like living with a human suspension bridge, strong enough to hold you steady, flexible enough to weather storms, and occasionally closed for maintenance without notice.

Yes, they can be overachieving perfectionists who disappear into their projects like they're tunneling for gold. And yes, their idea of romance might involve reorganizing your pantry or fixing your laptop instead of whispering sweet nothings. But here's the thing: when a 22 loves you, they build you into their vision. They make you part of the foundation, and that's a pretty sacred place to stand.

They may not always look like the Pinterest-perfect master planner you imagined. Sometimes they're more towel-and-mustard chaos than polished CEO. But that's the charm, they're deeply human while doing deeply important work. They'll forget to eat lunch but remember your long-term goals. They'll lose their keys but keep track of the ten-year plan for your family's future.

So, if you've got a 22 in your life, keep reminding them that they don't have to hold up the whole building alone. Offer a hand. Bring refreshments. Celebrate the wins and the mess. Because when a 22 feels safe, supported, and seen? They don't just build great things; they build great love.

If they feel they've messed up on something, gently remind them they are human. And it isn't failure; it's just a mess that needs a rinse and maybe a nap. Treat the mess as a symptom of deep engagement, instead of spiritual collapse; they come back faster, softer, and with more willingness to let you in.

And if you are a 22? Lighten up. Take breaks. Let someone else hold the blueprint for a while. The world will still be here when you get back, and your mustard-filled spoon will still be under that towel, so you can pick up where you left off.

**From a Life Path 22's perspective. Their perfect partner:**

Great Match. Easy flow, natural understanding; 2, 4, 8, 11, and 22.

Good Match. Supportive, friendly, promising; 6, 7, 9, and 44.

Ambitious Match. Full of potential but needs work; 1, 3, 5, and 33.

# Life Path 33/6: The Cosmic Healer in Yoga Pants and a Crown

They bring into being.

If the 11 is enlightenment on legs, and the 22 is God's project manager, then the 33 is the world's cosmic life coach, artist, and spiritual big sibling. They didn't just come here to love, heal, and inspire; they came to do it loudly. Not necessarily in volume (though some 33s can project across a crowded room), but in impact. This is the "Master Teacher," the person whose presence feels like a hug, a pep talk, and a slightly inconvenient mirror reflecting your full potential... all at once.

33 individuals are the spiritual nurturers of the world, part compassionate healer, part motivational speaker, and part emotional sponge. If you're a 33, you're likely the one everyone

turns to when the chips are down… and also when they just need someone to cry with during a sappy rom-com.

A 33's soul mission is to bring beauty, truth, and healing into form. That could mean creating art, raising consciousness, running a community center, writing songs that make people cry in the car, or giving advice so spot-on you wonder if they've been reading your diary. They are born with the urge to help, and if they're healthy and aligned, they help in ways that uplift, empower, and restore.

But let's not skip their very human side: the 33 can be a glorious mix of saintly intention and diva-level drama. They know they're special (oh, they know), and when they forget humility, their shadow side kicks in hard. This is when the cosmic healer begins to drift into the role of cosmic critic. "I'm only telling you this because I care," they'll say, while handing you a to-do list homework project for your soul you didn't ask for.

See, the 33s root number is the 6, the nurturer, the perfectionist, the home-and-heart guardian. That's where their need for beauty and harmony comes from. But that 6 energy also means they want things just so. And if they can't be perfect, they'll fake it so convincingly you'll never know the difference. The mask will be flawless, all smiles and reassurance, while behind the scenes they're stress-eating pita chips and Googling "how to save the world in under a week."

The truth is, even as kids, 33s have a vision. They see what could be better, prettier, more harmonious, and they want everyone to get on board. Sure, they might seem a little extra at times, but decades later, you'll look back and realize they weren't being difficult. They were auditioning for their role as *the Master Teacher of Earth,* and the playground was just their first classroom. Teachers often think 33 kids are natural leaders. And they are. But they're also perfectionists in training, which means they sometimes come off bossy. ("No, I'll pass out the crayons. I do it in rainbow order, so no one gets confused.")

The light side of a 33 is nothing short of magical. They're creative powerhouses, emotional first responders, and masters at making people feel seen. When they're grounded, their compassion is endless, and their art, whether literal art or the art of connection, can change lives. They have a knack for turning pain into beauty, chaos into clarity, and setbacks into stunning comebacks. They come equipped with a bottomless heart, an artistic streak that borders on divine inspiration, and a burning desire to leave the world better than they found it. They see suffering and immediately start scanning your soul for ways to fix it. You're creative, intuitive, and have an uncanny knack for making people feel seen, heard, and spiritually hugged. Even if it's just over text, people feel they have your full attention.

But being a 33 isn't all love and light. With great emotional power comes great responsibility, and sometimes a teensy tendency to feel taken advantage of. Their desire to serve can morph into guilt, burnout, or the all-too-familiar "I'll do it myself because no one else will do it right." That halo they're polishing can get heavy. Because they feel responsible for everything and everyone, they can slide into martyrdom faster than you can say "I'll do it myself." They can become controlling under the guise of "helping." And let's be honest, when they're stressed, they can be a little… superior. It's not intentional cruelty; it's just that they're convinced they know better. Which, annoyingly, they often do.

That being said, here's where that perfectionism becomes a superpower: if you're planning a huge event, wedding, retirement party, milestone celebration, or corporate launch, hire a 33 (or 6), if you can. Their vision is frighteningly clear, their standards are sky-high, and their attention to detail borders on psychic. You may find their "helpful notes" to loved ones, co-workers, or staff a tad stinging in the moment, but don't take it personally. That same exacting standard is what ensures that everything, the flowers, the timing, the playlist, the speeches, the emergency stash of safety pins, comes together flawlessly. The result will be better than you dared hope, and when it's all over, you'll be singing their praises… possibly while wondering if they secretly run the universe.

What makes them truly fascinating is the tension between their spiritual calling and their very human ego. Their life's work is to keep pulling that ego down from where seagulls fly and grounding it in humility, service, and genuine connection. When they do manage that, they're unstoppable. When they don't? They're still dazzling… just harder to live with.

If you're a 33, you didn't just show up on Earth to collect a paycheck and retire in a sensible zip code. Oh no, you came with a mission. A cosmic mission. One that probably involves healing, teaching, inspiring, rescuing, donating, elevating, or possibly doing all of that while holding someone else's emotional support cat.

Because you're wired for higher service, you tend to thrive in careers that let you feel useful in a soulful, heart-bursting, "I changed someone's life today" kind of way. Sure, your accountant friend may brag about spreadsheets and bonuses, but a 33? They're over restoring someone's faith in humanity, on their lunch break.

As the Master Teacher, they are compassionate, intuitive, wildly creative, and spiritually attuned beings who came to Earth with a heart three sizes too big and a to-do list longer than a CVS receipt. They're here to uplift humanity… and occasionally forget to eat lunch because they were busy helping you through your breakup (and your dog's separation anxiety).

When the 33 hits a rough patch, it can feel like the world's most nurturing lighthouse just short-circuited during a thunderstorm. You'll still see the light flickering, but now it's blinking in Morse code: "I'm fine, just saving humanity and crying into my tea!"

## How to Spot a 33 in the Wild

Clue: They're either saving you, improving you, or silently judging you, and sometimes all three at once.

You won't find a 33 yelling into their phone or aggressively cutting in line. Nope. These souls walk through life like emotional first responders, calm, kind, and always ready with an extra tissue or a perfectly timed "You're doing great, sweetie."

A true 33 can't not improve things. Their fingers itch for harmony. If you're at a friend's house party, the 33 is the one refolding the throws on the couch while carrying on a perfectly normal conversation about your love life. They'll "just help a little," and somehow, by the end of the night, the whole living room looks like a magazine spread.

They're also the person you'll catch doing small, thoughtful things without any fanfare, like putting water out for the delivery driver, fixing the jammed paper towel dispenser in a public restroom, or quietly slipping out to grab aspirin when someone mentions a headache.

Style-wise, they tend to dress in a way that feels both comfortable and curated, think coordinated colors, accessories that hold meaning, and a look that says, "I could run a meeting in this and then meditate under a tree." Even when they claim they "just threw something on," you can bet there was at least a passing thought about how the outfit would photograph.

Here's how to recognize one in their natural habitat:

**Gentle posture.** They lean in when you talk, as if your thoughts deserve center stage. No crossed arms or puffed-up egos, just open body language that says, "You're safe here."

**Soft gestures.** From sweeping hand motions that express big ideas to the occasional hand-to-heart moment, their gestures speak fluent empathy.

**Warm eye contact.** The kind of gaze that makes you want to confess your childhood secrets. Their eyes say, "I see you, I feel you, and I'm already thinking of ways to help you unpack that emotional baggage."

**Comforting movements.** They're the friend who rubs your back when you cry or gently touches your arm when you're spiraling. It's like emotional Reiki, and they don't even charge.

**Soothing tone.** Their voice? Velvet with a hint of herbal tea. If kindness had a sound, it would be a 33 whispering, "It's all going to be okay."

**Supportive body language.** They nod when you speak, tilt their head just slightly when you're struggling, and never, ever, check their phone mid-convo. They're present, patient, and possibly absorbing your feelings telepathically.

And if you ever see someone stepping in to lead without being asked, smoothing over tension between two people, or turning an ordinary gathering into a beautifully orchestrated experience… you've probably found your 33.

In short, if you've spotted one, count yourself lucky, you've just crossed paths with a natural-born healer who probably glows a little in moonlight.

## The Dating Style of a 33

"Love, light, and just a touch of "here's how you could do that better."

33s are like dating a spiritual guide, a therapist, an artist, and a cruise director all wrapped into one soulful, big-hearted human. You don't just get a partner; you get an experience. And yes, that experience will likely include a few gentle critiques of your life choices, but always "for your highest good," of course. They're not here to play games; they're here to heal, help, and hold your hand through the weird maze of life. Dating one can feel like being wrapped in emotional bubble wrap, tender, thoughtful, and protective. But behind that nurturing exterior is a person with dreams, desires, and the occasional need for a nap and comfort food.

From the very start, a 33 sees your potential. They see it before you do, and they will not let you forget it. You say you might want to start painting again? They're already researching art classes, buying you brushes, and suggesting a theme for your first gallery show. They are invested. And if you think that kind of enthusiasm will cool down after a few months... it won't. A 33 has this charming (and slightly intimidating) habit of finishing what they start, and they assume everyone else operates the same way. So, if you casually mentioned last week that you wanted to start painting, they will naturally assume you still want to paint this week. And next week. And possibly for the rest of your natural life. If you suddenly lose interest, they'll tilt their head and look at you the way you might look at an alien who just ran out of oxygen. The trick? Announce your momentary enthusiasms as exactly that: fleeting possibilities. Make it clear up front that your "I'm thinking about painting," isn't a soul contract. Their love is equal parts nurturing and inspiring. They want you to grow, and they want to grow with you. But let's be clear, "growing" to a 33 is not code for "hanging out and seeing where this goes." It's code for we're on a journey; there's a vision board involved, and I've already got the markers out.

At their best, they are the partner who cheers you on in every area of life, celebrates your wins like they're their own, and picks you up off the floor when you feel like quitting. They're in your corner, sleeves rolled up, ready to fight for you, or with you, if that's what it takes to get you back on track. (They mean well but just sayin'.)

Here's the catch: that same drive to improve things can slide right into over-managing the relationship. They might start subtly (or not-so-subtly) editing your wardrobe, your diet, your friend group, your morning routine, not out of malice, but because they truly believe they're helping you live your best life. If you're not careful, you could find yourself living inside their best life instead.

In love, they want deep connection and shared purpose. As parents, they're warm, inspiring, and may set the bar somewhere between "gifted" and "the next Dalai Lama." At work, they're inclusive leaders, intuitive problem-solvers, and secretly just trying to make the world more beautiful and loving, one caring task at a time.

Their dating style is emotionally intense in the most beautiful way, but it can be a lot for someone who just wants a low-maintenance relationship. They go deep, fast, and they'll want to talk about meaningful things. A quick "How was your day?" can turn into a three-hour conversation about your childhood dreams and how you're subconsciously blocking abundance.

If you're dating a 33, expect romance with purpose. They'll plan the perfect evening, but that evening might also double as a networking opportunity for your career, a fundraiser for a cause they care about, and a soft intervention for that "thing" they've noticed you've been avoiding. Boundaries are your friend here, and ironically, they'll respect you more for having them.

The good news? When they're grounded and healthy, loving a 33 is like living with your own personal cheerleader-meets-life-designer. They'll help you dream bigger, live more fully, and believe in yourself on days when you can barely get out of bed.

## Dating a 33: Masculine Edition

Dating a 33 man is like falling in love with the world's most devoted partner and most ambitious personal trainer, for your soul. They're part champion, part fixer, and part stage manager for the production of your best life. The love is real, the loyalty is fierce, and the desire to help you grow is unstoppable. The question is whether you can keep up without feeling like you're living inside a self-improvement documentary.

From the start, he moves with purpose. This isn't the "play it cool" type, if they like you, you'll know. They'll listen intently, remember everything you said, and start quietly laying the groundwork for a better, more beautiful life for both of you. They're romantic, yes, but their romance is often laced with practicality. Flowers are nice, but wouldn't you also like a new desk so you can finally finish that project you mentioned once in passing?

And here's the thing: as mentioned above, they will take your casual comments as commitments. If you say you want to run a 5K, they'll have you signed up for one by Thursday. Mention an interest in photography, and next week, a camera could be waiting for you with a detailed list of local classes. If you back out, expect that head tilt, that slightly baffled, slightly disappointed

*Debra Zachau*

look that says, How can you not want this anymore? We just talked about it!

They express love through action. They'll fix what's broken, plan what's next, and stand ready to defend you from anything that threatens your joy. But emotional expression? That can be trickier. They feel deeply, but they may default to doing rather than talking. If they can solve a problem for you, they will, even if what you actually needed was just a listening ear. Communication is key. They are psychic, but they are horrible mind readers.

Their standards are high, for themselves, for you, for the relationship. This can be inspiring when it motivates you to rise to your own potential… or exhausting if you're just trying to have a lazy Sunday without being "encouraged" into an educational outing. They don't mean to push; they genuinely believe they're helping. And to be fair, they usually are. But they also need to learn that love doesn't have to be a project.

When healthy, they are incredibly devoted partners. They'll champion your dreams, create stability, and bring beauty into your shared life. When stressed, they can tip into controlling behaviors, subtle criticism, or martyr mode ("I do everything for this relationship…"). They rarely realize they're doing it; they're just wired to make things better.

If you can accept their drive without taking it as judgment, and they can accept your boundaries without seeing them as rejection, 33 men becomes one of the most loyal, passionate, and visionary partners you could hope for. Just remember with them, "I might like to try this someday" should always be followed by, "but not yet, and maybe never." It'll save you both a lot of awkward moments and unused art supplies.

## So You've done it! You've fallen in love with a 33.

**DO:**

**Do recognize their vision.** If a 33 shares their dream for your shared life, they're not just idly chatting, they're already mentally decorating the reception hall. Meet them in that dream space, even if your only contribution right now is, "That sounds amazing."

**Do let them help you but set the boundaries.** They're natural fixers. If you don't need something "fixed," say so kindly and clearly. They'll respect honesty more than silent resentment.

**Do celebrate their standards.** Yes, their perfectionism can sting, but it's also the reason your birthday dinner looked like a five-star event instead of a last-minute pizza. Appreciate the upside of their high bar.

**Do tell them when you're in "idea only" mode.** If you mention wanting to start pottery "someday" and don't clarify, they'll have you signed up for classes, researching kiln rentals, and hosting your first pottery sale by Tuesday. Save yourself the awkward backpedal.

**Feed their need for beauty and meaning.** Whether it's flowers on the table or a meaningful conversation, they light up when their world feels harmonious and full of purpose.

**DON'T:**

**Don't dismiss their efforts.** If they spent hours planning something for you, even if it wasn't exactly what you wanted, appreciate the intention. They put love into it, and for a 33, that's a big deal.

**Don't confuse their guidance for criticism (every time).** Sometimes it is criticism. But often, it's a genuine belief that you can do something better. You don't have to agree, but don't assume it's an attack.

**Don't leave them guessing about your feelings.** They'll sense something's off and fill in the blanks themselves, usually with the most dramatic possibility. Save them (and yourself) from the emotional spiral.

**Don't ignore when they're overextending.** They'll burn themselves out trying to "do it all." Sometimes, the most loving thing you can do is hand them a cup of tea and tell them to sit down.

**Don't try to out-plan them.** You won't win. They've already thought of the angle you're about to bring up… twice.

Remember the loving, affirming voice they usually share with others? They forget to use it on themselves. Suddenly, nothing they do is enough (and neither are you, if you're too close to the emotional shrapnel). Eventually, they crash. Spiritually, physically, emotionally. You might find them wrapped in a blanket burrito, watching dog rescue videos while whispering, "I just need the planet to be okay."

Don't leave them like that because it's one of the only times they really don't think they have what it takes to enjoy and grow into their full life's potential. Get them a glass of wine, tell them you understand, and remind them that this awful feeling will pass. Oh, and if you're dating? Throw in a few kisses. They will remember and be forever grateful for this moment.

## Emergency Affirmations When Loving a 33.

(Best recited when they've reorganized your entire closet "as a gift" or given you a pep talk you didn't ask for.)

"They believe in me more than I believe in myself, and that's a gift."

"Their high standards come from love, not control."

"I can accept their help without losing my independence."

"Boundaries and gratitude can exist in the same sentence."

"Perfection is their comfort zone, but love is ours."

## The Spiritual Lessons of a 33 Life Path

33s are the "compassion artists" of numerology, but being a masterpiece comes with its share of smudges, touch-ups, and the occasional paint spill. Their soul contract is all about channeling their immense creative and healing gifts into something that uplifts others, without burning themselves to a crisp in the process. The challenge is that their deep sense of duty, paired with their perfectionist streak, can lead them to give so much that they accidentally erase themselves from the canvas. Part of their growth is learning that they can't, and shouldn't, try to fix everyone. They must understand that saying "no" to others can sometimes be saying "yes" to their own well-being, and that their value isn't measured solely by how much beauty, healing, or help they produce.

Humility is another big lesson for a 33. With the influence of the 6, the root number, the sense of responsibility along with the master number's drive for significance, can sometimes drift into "I know best" territory. Their evolution involves learning that the most powerful healing can come from simply listening, holding space, and letting others find their own way, even when it's not the path they would have chosen. They also need to make peace with imperfection, both in themselves and others, and understand that flaws don't diminish worthiness.

When a 33 steps into their highest potential, they become a walking example of how love, creativity, and vision can change lives. They inspire others to dream big and follow through, showing that beauty and practicality can co-exist. They demonstrate the power of showing up for people without keeping score and prove that kindness is not weakness. A fully realized 33 can awaken something in others, sparking their belief in their own ability to create, heal, and rise above mediocrity. In short, a 33s greatest lesson is learning how to give without losing themselves, and their greatest gift is teaching the art of showing up for life with equal parts heart and skill. They're not here to save everyone, just to offer their gifts, their wisdom, and their love in ways that empower others to save themselves.

So, what have we learned about our dazzling, slightly bossy, and occasionally overextended 33? First, they are walking Pinterest boards, they see the beauty, they design the beauty, and then they call three vendors and have the beauty delivered by Tuesday. They are the people you want planning your wedding, your retirement party, and possibly your funeral (especially your funeral), which will, naturally, have tasteful floral arrangements and a killer playlist.

Yes, they can be a little intense. Yes, they may stare at you blankly when you abandon last week's "I want to take up painting" phase, mostly because they've started following a Bob Ross fan page on your behalf. But underneath the perfectionist frosting and occasional "I know best" sprinkles, a 33's heart is pure gold.

When they're at their best, they show us how to dream big without losing our grip on reality, how to show up for others without keeping a tally, and how to make life more beautiful without waiting for permission. Dating, working with, or just being friends with a 33 means you get front-row seats to a show where compassion, creativity, and competence all share the stage. Just remember: if you don't want to be swept into their next big project, keep your random "wouldn't it be fun if..." thoughts to yourself.

They thrive when they can inspire, guide, nurture, and create, but they struggle when they forget they're human too. Their dark side? Perfectionism dressed up as helpfulness, martyrdom disguised as responsibility, and a tendency to carry the emotional weight of the entire planet... plus five close friends and a distant cousin.

If you're in a relationship with a 33, here's the thing: You will never be bored. You will never be unchallenged. And you will probably never again get away with half-assing your dreams, because the 33 won't let you forget you have them.

**From a Life Path 33's perspective. Their perfect partner:**

Great Match. Easy flow, natural understanding; 3, 6, and 9.

Good Match. Supportive, friendly, promising; 2, 4, and 8.

Ambitious Match. Full of potential but needs work; 1, 5, 7, and 11.

A Neutral Match. Could go either way, depends on maturity; 22, 44, and 33.

# 44

# Life Path 44/8: The Masterful Visionary Who Needs a Vacation.

We've arrived at 44, the cosmic CEO of the numerology world, the kind of person who can turn a vague idea into a Fortune 500 business plan before breakfast. Part visionary guru, part relentless achiever, and wholly unstoppable, at least until they run out of coffee. After that, they still go, but in a crankier fashion. These are the spiritual architects who blend practicality with purpose, dream big but also hand you a fully detailed execution plan with deadlines, contingencies, all backed up in the cloud. Rarely does a 44 see a goal they can't conquer through sheer willpower. Responsibility isn't something they do, it's part of their DNA. Friends trust them more than their GPS (and honestly, the GPS could take a few pointers). Their self-discipline borders on legendary; it's said they can walk past a dozen donuts in the break room without that stupid fake cheerleading voice in their heads.

They have the mental endurance of a marathoner, the focus of a brain surgeon, and the stubborn resolve of a toddler who's just learned the word "No."

But every powerhouse has its quirks. The 44s shadow side often shows up as a brand of stubbornness that could be patented. They can be a touch impatient (pacing aggressively when the microwave takes too long), and they're not famous for loving last-minute changes. Even though their way is usually brilliant, it's not always the only way, but good luck convincing them of that in the heat of the moment. Their inner critic can sometimes shout louder than the rest of the room. Sometimes their inner critic can get too loud, and their overwork ethic could burn them out faster than a cheap candle.

Still, they are the rare unicorns of the numerology world, powerful, intuitive, grounded, deeply responsible, and here to marry the spiritual with the material. They take relationships seriously, often sticking around longer than most, even though they hate drama in all its messy forms. They're conflict avoiders, preferring calm and steady waters, but they are also quietly attentive to the needs of the people they care about. Just don't shout those needs at them. If you do, they'll walk away... far, far away... both literally and figuratively. Life with a 44 means you get a partner, friend, or coworker who will help build the life you dream about, as long as you're willing to hand them the blueprints and keep the coffee coming.

As kids, they were the miniature project managers of the playground. While other kids were happily eating paste or learning to whistle, 44s were making sandcastle blueprints and assigning roles sounding like, "You dig, you haul, I'll supervise." They had a knack for seeing how things should be done, and more importantly, making sure they were done. Their toy shelves were organized by size and purpose (at least until someone messed it up, at which point they'd reorganize the entire room to cope with the chaos). Even at a young age, they had a quiet sense of responsibility that made teachers trust them with things like handing out homework sheets or keeping an eye on the class hamster. And yes, they took that job seriously. They were also early masters of delayed gratification, the kind of kids who could save the last cookie "for later" without touching it, which baffled their sugar-high peers. That said, they didn't just follow rules; they made them and might have enforced them with the solemnness of a traffic cop. Childhood for a 44 was equal parts leadership training and learning how to deal with the maddening unpredictability of everyone else.

In relationships of all kinds, romantic partners, friends, coworkers, or family, they approach people the way they approach projects: with commitment, loyalty, and a plan for how to make things better. They don't collect "casual" connections like some people collect Instagram followers; instead, they invest their energy in fewer, but deeper, bonds. When you're in a 44s circle, you can count on them to show up, and not just physically, but mentally and emotionally, too.

In friendships, they're the steady one who remembers your big interview date, ask about it afterward, and celebrate your wins like they're their own. In the workplace, they're the reliable teammate who hits deadlines and keeps a cool head when others are panicking (though inside, they might be silently muttering about your time management skills). With love partners, they're long-haul people. They're not in it for the drama; they're in it for the building of trust, of shared goals, and yes, sometimes of actual dream houses.

That said, they can be a little...how do I put it... intense. They have high standards and assume others share them, so when a friend flakes or a coworker drops the ball, their inner "quality control inspector" can flare up. They're also not big on emotional theatrics; if you're looking for someone to throw a drink in your honor during a fight, keep walking. But if you want someone who will stand by you, quietly fix the problem, and make sure it doesn't happen again, you've found your person.

They're equal parts visionary guru and disciplined taskmaster; think Oprah meets a NASA flight director, only with more sticky notes and fewer commercial breaks. They are the rare blend of practicality, creativity, and laser-focused determination. Where most of us see chaos, they see bullet points, a color-coded spreadsheet, and an inspirational quote taped to the fridge for motivation. And if all else fails, they've got DoorDash on speed dial, because even visionaries need tacos.

What makes them particularly magnetic is their ability to turn massive, sprawling ideas into real, tangible results. You may look at an ambitious plan and say, "That'll take a miracle." A 44, however, will calmly reply, "No problem, I'll have it done by Tuesday." Efficiency and productivity are their love languages. They practically hum with satisfaction when they tick boxes off a list, and teamwork can be one of their strong suits, provided, of course, that they're the ones directing the team.

Here's where things get funny: delegation is their kryptonite. It's not that they don't trust you, it's that they trust their own system more. If you want something done right, they'll just do it themselves… which is how they end up missing vacations, family events, or that yoga retreat everyone begged them to try. The irony is, they often don't realize how much pressure this puts on those around them. Friends and family quietly pray for less structure and a little more spontaneity but suggesting that to them can feel like asking a surgeon to "just wing it."

The truth is, the mature 44, the one who has learned to loosen the grip on the wheel and occasionally "play it by ear", is unstoppable in the best way. They balance their drive with compassion, their ambition with humility, and their endless goals with actual human connection. And this is the sweet spot, because while it's true that all Life Paths thrive once they become self-aware, for a 44 it's transformative. Once they realize how their words land, whether they're uplifting, inspiring, or accidentally flattening everyone around them, they can step into their role not just as the architect of empires, but as the builder of hearts, too.

If they were a movie character, they'd be part Tony Stark, part Marie Kondo, part Desmond Tutu, with a hint of Hermione Granger's planner obsession. They're the cosmic overachievers who came to Earth with a to-do list titled "Make the world better," and they're checking it off, one step at a time. They are grounded visionaries with a steel spine and a soft heart. They dream big, plan bigger, and have the stamina to pull it all off twice. Whether they're managing a team, building an empire, or folding laundry with architectural precision, they bring excellence to everything they touch. Underneath all that structure and success? A deeply empathetic soul who genuinely wants to leave things better than they found them. They're not just here to climb the ladder; they're installing elevators and making sure everyone gets a ride to the top.

## How to Spot a 44 in the Wild

If you've ever wondered what it looks like when determination puts on a pair of shoes and walks into a room, that's your 44. You don't even have to ask their birthday; you'll feel their energy before they open their mouth. Here's how to recognize one when you stumble across this rare species:

**Confident Posture.** A 44 doesn't slouch. They stand tall, chest out, like they've just been appointed Director of the Universe. Their body language broadcasts, "I've got this handled", and they usually do. If they're leaning on a desk, it's not laziness; it's strategy.

**Firm Gestures.** Watch their hands. Their gestures are crisp, decisive, and punctuated, as if their body is underlining their words in bold font. If you ever see a 44 fidgeting, check for signs of fever; they're not themselves if they're appearing unsure.

**Direct Eye Contact.** They don't just look at you; they laser-beamy into your soul. Their gaze is unwavering, like they're already building a three-step plan for your life while you're still talking about what you had for breakfast. It can feel slightly unnerving, but also, oddly motivating.

**Purposeful Movements.** Nothing is wasted on them. They don't just walk across a room; they power-stride. Every step has a destination, every action an outcome. Watching them is like watching a productivity poem in motion.

**Assertive Tone.** When they speak, people listen. Their voice carries authority without even trying, like a teacher who doesn't need to raise her voice because the class already knows who's in charge. They sound like they were born with a built-in microphone.

**Task-Oriented Body Language.** Look for arms crossed like a project manager waiting for you to finish your part. Notice the frequent glances at their watch, the subtle tapping of a pen, or that faint "let's move this along" energy radiating off them. They carry an air of urgency, even while drinking chamomile tea. Especially while drinking chamomile.

**Bonus Tell.** If you see someone glaring at the microwave because the timer says "0:27" and it still feels too slow, congratulations, you've spotted a 44 in their natural habitat.

## Dating Style of a 44

When it comes to dating, they show up like they're launching a romantic startup. They're not here for chaos; they're here to build something meaningful, sustainable, and preferably with a five-year plan. They're drawn to partners who are equally purpose-driven, someone with ambition, integrity, and a shared vision of the future. If you dream of building a tiny house off-grid while launching a social enterprise, you might just be their soulmate.

Practical and grounded, they approach relationships like they approach everything else: thoughtfully and thoroughly. They're problem-solvers who'd rather talk things through than let issues fester. That is, if uncontrollable crying, whining, and yelling aren't present. If they are, you'll find your 44 in the garage or office with every door locked, waiting until the emotional storm has passed. You'll rarely catch them ghosting, unless their phone's battery dies mid-schedule.

Their style is deliberate and unmistakably intentional. Expect them to be ready on time, dressed like they've already met your parents, and armed with a list of questions that sound like a job interview: "Where do you see yourself in five years? Do you recycle? How do you feel about legacy projects?" This isn't cold; it's not wanting to waste time dating the wrong person. They're not trying to scare you off; they're just filtering out anyone who isn't ready for a capital-S Serious Relationship.

Romantic gestures? Oh, they have them, but always with a practical spin. They'll surprise you with a weekend getaway, but it will include an itinerary, a budget breakdown, and perhaps laminated maps. They'll buy you jewelry, but it will come with an insurance policy. And when they finally say, "I love you," rest assured, they mean it, they've done the math, and they've already considered the long-term tax implications.

But here's the catch: they can overdo it. Between work, world-improvement projects, and perfecting their gluten-free sourdough, they may forget to rest, or, you know, cuddle. Their perfectionism can sneak into the relationship, turning "quality time" into an evaluation session. Luckily, they're just as committed to personal growth as they are to your couple goals. With the right partner (someone patient, nurturing, and willing to pry the laptop out of their hands), they can be loyal, passionate, and beautifully devoted.

## Dating a 44: Masculine Edition

Dating a 44 man is like signing up for a masterclass in commitment. This guy doesn't just "date", he strategically invests in relationships. Forget casual flings; he's building an empire and wants a partner who can co-sign the blueprint. If he asks you out, it's not because he was bored on a Tuesday, it's because he's consulted his gut, and decided you're worth his time.

He shows up polished, punctual, and ready to impress, not in a showy, peacock kind of way, but in an "I've ironed my shirt, researched the restaurant, and secured reservations" kind of way. He's the type to ask what your favorite dessert is and then have it waiting at the table. Thoughtful? Absolutely. Overprepared? Quite possibly.

They court with purpose. He listens carefully, remembers small details, and turns them into grand gestures. Mention once that you've always wanted to visit Italy? Expect a casual follow-up about his "future travel fund." Say you like sunflowers? Don't be surprised if he turns up with a bouquet and a plan to plant a garden together. His goal isn't just to win your heart; it's to build a long-term partnership brick by brick.

But here's the catch: perfectionism sneaks in. He may overanalyze every text, reread your last message four times, and take three days to craft the "perfect" reply (while you're thinking, buddy, just send the emoji already). He's prone to treating dates like board meetings, structured, intentional, and a little intense.

Looseness, spontaneity, and "winging it" don't always come naturally.

Yet once you're in his orbit, you'll find the 44 man is deeply loyal, protective, and invested in your shared future. He's not out to waste time; he's here to create a love story that doubles as a legacy.

## I see you have chosen a Life Path 44

**DO:**

**Do respect their time.** Their calendar is in ink, and if you're late, they'll already be calculating how many productive minutes they've lost. They most likely won't say anything but will take note and watch to see if it becomes a pattern.

**Do share your goals.** Nothing excites them more than a partner with a vision. Bonus points if your dream can be outlined with timelines. Bring your dreams to the table, and you won't find a better person to champion you to success.

**Do appreciate their effort.** If they've planned the perfect date, from the dinner reservation to the playlist in the car, don't brush it off. That's love, 44-style. Speak up. It's not that they need it all the time, but to keep things like this coming, acknowledge them for their efforts.

**Do encourage downtime.** Sometimes they need a reminder that rest is not weakness. Suggest a spontaneous weekend away, or at least a nap. As mentioned earlier, as one of the shadows of the root 8, work is their fun, and they really have a hard time regulating themselves with balanced self-care.

**Do admire their discipline.** If they pass up the donuts in the break room, clap. If they finish a project ahead of schedule, clap louder. Applaud like they've landed a Mars rover in your backyard. Forget flowers or candy, what they secretly want is someone to notice that they hit every goal on their to-do list and washed the car. A little admiration goes a long way with a 44.

**DON'T:**

**Don't bring chaos.** Chaos makes them twitchy. Messy schedules, forgotten reservations, or a car that's running on "we'll find gas eventually" vibes? It's basically their nightmare. To them, structure equals peace. When you bring chaos, it's like dumping a bag of live squirrels onto their keyboard. Don't do it.

**Don't dismiss their intensity.** Yes, they care a lot. About everything. Their job, their family, their recycling bin, saving the whales, saving you from yourself, it's all important. You may be tempted to tease them with a casual, "Relax, it's not that deep," but here's the truth: for them, it is that deep. Their intensity is part of their DNA and dismissing it will feel like telling Mozart to "tone it down with the piano." Their passion is their charm; it's what makes them magnetic. If you can't handle the fire, step away from the 44.

**Don't expect last-minute plans.** It's worth saying again, a 44 doesn't "do" spontaneous. If you want a Friday night date, you'd better get it on the books by Tuesday. They're not being cold, they just don't want their perfectly balanced week derailed by "Oh, by the way, let's go camping right now." To them, spontaneity feels less like fun and more like someone just yanked the emergency brake on their life plan. Give them notice. Give them time to prepare. They'll show up in style, fully ready to enjoy themselves, once it's been scheduled.

**Don't mistake their focus for coldness.** They can stare at their laptop for hours without blinking, and yes, it looks a little robotic. But don't assume that just because they're knee-deep in spreadsheets, they've stopped caring about you. Sometimes their way of showing love is building an empire that pays the bills. Their focus is love in disguise: every late night, every "just one more email" is often a sacrifice they're making for the bigger picture. If you mistake this for coldness, you'll miss the point entirely. They're not ignoring you, they're building you a castle.

**Don't shout at them.** If you feel like yelling, save your breath. Loud, emotional outbursts make a 44 vanish faster than a magician's rabbit. They'll retreat to the garage, the office, or the nearest room with a door they can lock. They don't thrive on conflict; they avoid it like cats avoid water. If you really want to reach them, keep your voice calm and your words measured. With that, they will turn off all distractions and listen.

### Emergency Affirmations when Loving a 44

Being with one can feel like being invited onto a high-speed train, one with purpose, direction, and an exact arrival time. If you're along for the ride, affirmations can keep you grounded, centered, and a little more forgiving when their intensity outpaces your Sunday nap energy.

"I bring balance, not chaos."

"Their intensity is passion, not pressure."

"It's okay to be spontaneous in my own way."

"Behind the discipline is devotion."

"I don't need to shout to be heard."

## Spiritual Lessons for the 44 Life Path.

They are here to marry the spiritual and the material. Their job is to prove that practical doesn't mean boring, and divine doesn't mean floaty. They are the architects of sacred systems. When they trust their intuition and release the crushing pressure to be perfect, miracles can move through them like blueprints from the divine.

But they aren't here to simply build empires of concrete and skyscrapers. Their spiritual lesson is to learn vulnerability, the art of asking for help, letting go of control, and realizing that carrying the weight of the world alone is not the same thing as leadership. They're here to understand that while discipline is a gift, flexibility is wisdom. And that sometimes, surrendering to the flow creates greater success than sticking to the plan with white-knuckled determination.

What they are here to teach the rest of us is just as profound. They show us that spirituality doesn't have to live in temples or yoga studios; it can exist in boardrooms, balance sheets, and business plans. They remind us that "practical" can be sacred, and that building systems, businesses, and communities with integrity is just as holy as meditation on a mountaintop. They teach that success without soul is hollow, and soul without structure will collapse. Through their example, they invite us to blend discipline with devotion, purpose with play, and ambition with compassion.

So, while a 44 may look like the no-nonsense builder of the Universe, underneath that polished exterior is a soul reminding us all that heaven and earth aren't two separate destinations, they're meant to meet right here, in the lives we're creating every day.

**From a Life Path 44s perspective. Their perfect partner:**

Great Match. Easy flow, natural understanding;  4, 8, 22, and 44.

Good Match. Supportive, friendly, promising; 2, 6, 7, and 9.

Ambitious Match. Full of potential but needs work; 1, 3, 5, and 11.

A Neutral Match. Could go either way, depends on maturity; 33.

# A note about 44 and 55 Life Paths.

Before we dive into the wild ride that is  55, let me pause and tell you something important: 44s and 55s are the unicorns of numerology. They're rare. I've worked with thousands of people, and I've met some 44/8s, but 55s? I've met exactly one. One. A single, lightning-bolt client whose session left me thinking, "Yep, this deserves its own chapter."

Naturally, I went looking for more. I did what any curious researcher does: I Googled "famous 55 people." And guess what I found? A list of celebrities who, after doing the math myself, weren't 55s at all. Not even close. Jamie Lee Curtis, (November 22, 1958), is a Life Path 11, *not 55*. Daniel Day-Lewis, (April 29, 1957) is a 37/1. Ernest Hemingway, (July 21, 1899)? Also a 37/1. So, if you think you've stumbled across a 55, please, for the love of numerology, do your own math before you start shouting about it on social media. (Which is a tough crowd if you get something wrong.)

Now, here's where things get interesting to number nerds. Life Paths 44 and 55 filter information in ways the rest of us simply don't. The 44 processes with a closed-minded certainty, convinced they're holding the one and only manual for "How life works." The 55? They process on an entirely different plane. Their thinking is so abstract that people instinctively back away... but never actually leave the room, because everyone knows brilliance is happening, they just can't quite figure out what form it's going to take.

The trouble is, 55s aren't like the rest of us. If you're expecting a tidy breakdown of strengths, weaknesses, and hobbies, forget it. They are double 5s: restless, distractible, forever chasing the next shiny idea. Mix that with a 1's headstrong, action-oriented freaks (cool freaks), and you've got someone who doesn't always "play well with others." These are not the teammates who show up early with refreshments and an organized agenda. They're the ones who disappear for three weeks, then return with the one solution no one else could have dreamed of. You (a comparatively normal person) will likely end up doing the household chores or running the business errands because your 55 is too busy reinventing the wheel and making it faster.

And yet, here's the kicker: when a 55 does finish a project, the results are staggering. Pure brilliance. Genius, even. They can't be matched in originality or spark. But living with one? It's like raising a five-year-old with a PhD. They're critical thinkers, but if they don't develop compassion early, that brainpower becomes a battering ram. Without guidance, they can be destructive, not because they want to be, but because their fire burns so hot that they scorch everyone in the vicinity.

So, yes, they are the aliens among us. They don't follow the same rules. They don't think the same way. You, as a student of numerology, can throw out everything you've learned so far about Life Path dynamics when dealing with one. They're here for big things, different things. They'll give great counsel if you're ready to hear it, but if you dismiss them, they're gone. Door slammed. Conversation over.

Raising or loving a 55 is not for the faint of heart. You'll need patience, boundaries, and a good sense of humor. You'll need to teach them that ego doesn't have to sit at the head of the table and that compassion is just as valuable as critical thought. If they can master those lessons, their contribution to the world is immeasurable. If not, well, buckle up. The ride will be wild, unpredictable, and possibly destructive. But one thing's for sure: it won't be boring.

55

# Life Path 55: The Firecrackers of Numerology.

If they had a theme song, it would be something snappy with a driving beat and a chorus that screams, "Don't fence me in!" That is, if you can find one. These individuals are walking, talking bottle rockets, bursting with energy, creativity, and a relentless thirst for life. They don't just want to live; they want to experience everything and then talk about it passionately over coffee with a stranger they've just met on a train to somewhere exciting.

They are natural adventurers, always seeking the next thrill, whether it's a spontaneous trip abroad, a new career, or a creative project they've just dreamt up and might actually start tomorrow, or right now (just give them a minute). They are deeply freedom-loving, often breaking away from expectations or norms to forge their own winding, scenic path. Visionary and creative, they not only dream big, they feel big, and they express themselves in colorful, artistic, or wildly original ways that may leave more grounded folks slightly dizzy, but impressed, nonetheless.

Communication is their superpower. They're eloquent, quick-witted, and can talk their way into or out of just about anything. Their intuition is finely tuned, and they're usually guided by a deep inner knowing, which, while occasionally baffling to outsiders, tends to be spookily accurate. Flexible and adaptable, they pivot gracefully through life's changes, and their self-motivation drives them even when no one else is watching. Optimistic to their core, they're the type of people who believe tomorrow might just be the day their wildest dream comes true. Add a layer of empathy, and you get someone who genuinely wants others to succeed as well. They just might encourage you to quit your job and move to Cancun to do it. (Which makes them a cool ass friend but, just lettin' ya know in advance).

I gotta be honest, life with a 55 isn't always smooth sailing. That same hunger for freedom and novelty can leave them restless, like they're always one step away from their next big thing. They're not known for sitting still, which can make relationships, jobs, or long-term projects tricky to maintain. Impulsiveness is a double-edged sword: brilliant in moments of genius innovation, but potentially disastrous when paired with a credit card and late-night flight deals.

Unpredictability comes with the territory, making them fascinating but sometimes making it hard to rely on them. Recklessness can rear its head when they charge forward without considering the consequences, and a touch of selfishness may emerge when their personal desires overshadow collective goals.

Commitment might feel like a cage to a 55, and their disorganized tendencies mean they can have five projects in motion and forget where they put their phone during every single one of them. Overindulgence is another possible pitfall (they don't just enjoy life, they devour it), and patience? Let's just say that's a skill they may develop later in life, only if they feel it necessary.

Despite their challenges, they are vibrant, magnetic, and unforgettable. They're here to shake things up, inspire change, and remind us all that life is meant to be lived out loud, with passion, curiosity, and the occasional plot twist. Just buckle up because with a 55, it's going to be one heck of a ride.

They are job-hopping, joy-chasing, change-loving dynamos. Their resume is also seen as the professional equivalent of channel surfing with purpose. If you're a 55, chances are you've rewritten your resume more times than you've changed your passwords, and each version probably includes at least one wild surprise. But that's not a flaw, it's your genius!

They crave freedom, variety, and excitement. The traditional 9 to 5 cubicle life? Not unless the cubicle has a zipline from the fifth-floor window to the car. This is the Life Path of the visionary explorer, the fast-talking entrepreneur, the last-minute flight-booking storyteller who's allergic to monotony.

Being adaptable and resourceful, 55s are natural entrepreneurs. One day, they're launching a podcast from a hammock in the backyard, and the next, they're beta-testing an app to help people meditate while skydiving. Freelancing suits them like a glove, or better yet, like a glove that turns into a scarf, hat, or side hustle depending on the mood.

Careers that allow flexibility, travel, or creative expression tend to bring out the best in a 55. Think travel blogger, artist, life coach, social media influencer, consultant, DJ, PR wizard, event caterer, or digital nomad in general. Basically, if it comes with variety and a little chaos, they're in. Does it involve routine, repetition, or excessive paperwork? You can count them out.

But don't mistake their freedom-loving nature for irresponsibility. When a 55 is passionate about what they do, they're unstoppable. They'll charm, dazzle, pitch, write, create, problem-solve, and reinvent entire industries if given the space to breathe it into the world.

Sure, they may occasionally ghost a job faster than a bad Tinder date, but it's not because they're lazy. It's because deep down, they know they're meant to live fully, love wildly, and work in ways that inspire, not just require.

## How to Spot a 55 in the Wild

Ah, hello elusive one. Part wanderer, part whirlwind, all charisma. If you're trying to identify one in the wild, skip the spreadsheets and just follow the sound of laughter, the scent of spontaneity, or the sparkle trail of glitter metaphorically (or literally) falling from their wake. A 55 rarely blends in. Their posture is relaxed, often leaning back like they've got all the time in the world, even if they're five minutes from hopping a plane or hosting a meeting. Their gestures are fluid, animated, and spontaneous, much like an Italian family after a bit of wine.

Their eye contact? Curious and magnetic. Like they're scanning your soul to see if you too, might be up for a spontaneous cross-country road trip or funding a pop-up art installation in a desert. You'll notice movement, a lot of it. They bounce, they sway, they tap their foot to music no one else hears. Energy radiates from them like a phone with 10 browser tabs open and a playlist called "Let's make life interesting."

They speak with passion, infusing even the most mundane topics with flair. ("Okay, but imagine if breakfast cereal was also a podcast...") And their body language is playful, looking you in the eye when intrigued, throwing in a mock drum solo, or casually dancing down the grocery aisle. For no reason. Other than joy.

So, if you spot someone who seems part philosopher, part party guest, and part pirate captain with a plan, congratulations, you've just witnessed a 55 in their natural habitat: anywhere exciting.

## Dating a 55: Love on the Loose (But in a good way).

Dating a 55 is like falling headfirst into a spontaneous road trip where nobody packed snacks, but somehow you're still having the time of your life. These free spirits are fueled by curiosity, creativity, and a near-unstoppable craving for new experiences. If there were a dating app filter for "must love mystery, adventure, and existential karaoke," they'd swipe right in a heartbeat. They don't do cookie-cutter courtship. Forget flowers and a movie, try a surprise drum circle on the beach or a Tuesday night trip to a UFO-themed diner. Their hearts beat to a different rhythm, one that demands both connection and breathing room. Translation: they'll love you deeply, as long as you don't try to chain them to a dinner with the (fill in the blank...neighbors, in-laws, friends) every weekend.

They're creative lovers and inventive partners, always coming up with ways to keep things playful, fresh, and emotionally alive. But underneath that whirlwind charm is a need for a partner who can provide a sense of grounding. They may not admit it out loud, but they benefit from someone who gently tethers them to reality without stifling their spark.

## Dating a 55: Masculine Edition

Dating him is not so much a relationship as an adventure subscription service. If he has money, expect spontaneous flights to places you didn't even know existed, "Pack a bag, babe, we're going to Reykjavik tonight." If he doesn't, it's still spontaneous, just more like glow-in-the-dark bowling, 3 a.m. escape rooms, or sudden rounds of golf at an obscure course three towns over. Either way, your calendar is toast. Schedules? He's never heard of them. Kids' ballet recital? Your boss's retirement dinner? Christmas morning? All of these are apparently negotiable if he's suddenly inspired to chase the Northern Lights.

It's not that he doesn't love you. He does. He just can't sit still. The man treats boredom like it's a mortal sin. Being alone with his thoughts feels like being locked in a room with a ticking time bomb, so he fills the silence with activity, motion, and distraction. He's got a restless energy that demands engagement, travel, hobbies, projects, or a new passion that will probably shift three more times before the end of the weekend.

Now, here's the deal: if you're a person who lives and dies by a schedule, if you love your calendar, meal prep Sundays, and the sacred 9 p.m. bedtime, this relationship will test your soul. You'll either learn to surrender and roll with the chaos, or you'll spend the relationship muttering under your breath while boarding yet another surprise flight in the wrong shoes that you didn't have time to pack properly. But if you do lean into it? If you let him sweep you up in his tornado of spontaneity, you'll experience life in vivid, unpredictable Technicolor. He'll expand your world in ways you never imagined, forcing you to be present, daring, and uncomfortably adventurous.

So, the real question is: can you drop everything at a moment's notice, laugh at the madness, and say yes to boarding that plane? If not, swipe left before he steals your heart.

Fueled by freedom, they make brilliant storytellers, adventurers, artists, and accidental philosophers. They're the friend who disappears for six months and comes back with a tattoo, a business idea, and a new lease on life (sometimes all acquired in one weekend).

But they're not just chaos in cute shoes, they're visionaries with heart. When they care, they care deeply. When they commit (and yes, it can happen), they bring passion, creativity, and a whole suitcase of innovative solutions. They crave partners who won't try to tame them but will dance beside them in the whirlwind. Sure, they can be impulsive. Sometimes flaky. Occasionally allergic to planning. But they also remind us that joy matters. That change is necessary. That growth is supposed to feel like an adventure, not a chore.

## Spiritual Lessons of the Life Path 55

If the 44 is the architect, the 55 is the storm. These rare souls didn't exactly come to Earth to master structure, calendars, or planners. Honestly, they didn't even come here to like them. The truth is, 55s are here to learn the hardest lesson of all: how to live with humans who insist on alarm clocks, traffic laws, and PTA meetings. While everyone else builds routines, they're busy dismantling them, half the time just to see what happens.

At their core, they came here to wrestle with one very human challenge: restraint. Not to kill their spark, but to realize that not every impulse deserves immediate execution. Can they pause before booking a one-way ticket to Bali at 2 a.m.? Or at least remember to book travel insurance in case they change their minds? Can they sit still long enough to let someone else finish a sentence? Can they remember that other people actually need notice before their lives get turned upside down? Either way they play it, the ride will be worth it for them. But what about the other people in their lives?

Learning patience, responsibility, and respect for other people's sense of order is their soul curriculum. It's not about becoming "normal" (that's never going to happen), but while the 55 wrestles with structure, they're here to remind the rest of us that our structures are cages more often than they are safety nets. They teach us how to break free of the rules that don't serve us, how to say yes when life invites us to play, and how to risk comfort in exchange for experience.

The 55 soul whispers (okay, shouts), "Stop waiting. Stop stalling. Stop overthinking. Live!" They push us toward the edge of spontaneity, daring us to trust that joy can be found in the unplanned, the risky, the unpredictable.

They are here to prove that freedom is sacred, and that when you stop trying to control every detail, you make room for magic. Yes, they may drive us insane in the process, but they also crack open doors to worlds we never would've walked through on our own. Leaving us thinking to ourselves, "If I survive this, it's gonna make a great story!".

Yes, they're exhausting. Yes, you will lose count of unfinished projects around the house (seriously, don't even look in the garage). But you'll also find yourself laughing at midnight while laying on an airport floor, hiking trails you didn't know existed, and realizing that "sensible" may not be the only way to do life.

The spiritual lesson for the rest of us? Stop waiting for permission. Stop holding onto safety rails. Let the 55s, (the few who are around), drag us into a life that's bigger, bolder, and a whole lot messier.

So, raise a glass (they probably already ordered one for you). Love them, forgive them, and try to keep up, because when you're in the orbit of a 55, you'll never forget it.

## Okay, About the Match Chart.

Well to be honest, I'm looking at it, and feel I must ask you not to hold me to any of this because we are dealing with a wonderful wildcard. I will give you my reasons for my answers as a bonus.

**Great Match.** Easy flow, natural understanding; 2, (because of their dedication to their partners). 5, (as they are just as ambitious and full of sparkle as 55s).

**Good Match.** Supportive, friendly, promising; 1, (if their ambition is pointed in the same direction. If not there will be a ton of competition, but if emotions stay in check, it's a good match). 7, (isn't likely to participate in all the travel a 55 will want to do, they will stay loyal but won't miss them when they're gone, leaving both refreshed after the break).

**Ambitious Match.** Could go either way, depends on maturity; 4, (needs security). 6, (needs control, and there's no controlling our 55). 8, (needs to stay in one place long enough to build something). 9, (is the legacy builder full of keepsakes and memories but will tend to want to nest more than a 55).

**A Neutral Match.** Could go either way, depends on maturity; 3, (communication will be good, but I don't think a 55 will allow a 3 to enjoy their own creativity. 55s will want to embellish, improve, and blow up what's started by the 3, leaving them feeling disillusioned).

# In Closing

So, here we are at the end of this numerology ride. I've shared with you what I've learned, first by studying the traditional definitions, then by dragging those numbers out of the textbooks and into the messy, unpredictable, very human world. And yes, most of the classic traits hold water. But let's be honest: if you've ever flipped through a numerology book and read a passage that made you go "Huh?" you're not alone. I've done the same. That's why I set out to compare what's been written with what actually shows up in real life, through my experience.

Here's what I've discovered: numerology, at its best, is the most solid framework for human nature I've ever studied. It explains why people are the way they are, not just what they do, but the deeper wiring underneath. And once you can see the why, life gets a whole lot easier. You stop taking things so personally. You realize your coworker isn't stubborn just to spite you; they were born a 4, which practically requires them to wrestle with cement blocks of certainty before they budge an inch. You understand your partner's constant need for variety isn't a character flaw, it's their 5 showing. And you finally get that your own quirks aren't proof of being "broken", they're just the instructions stamped on your soul's operating system. In other words, "part of your charm."

Numerology doesn't excuse bad behavior, but it helps you tell the difference between a natural-born quirk and something negotiable. That's the magic. You stop wasting energy trying to sandpaper people into shapes they were never meant to be. You start asking better questions. Is this trait essential to who they are, or is this just a defense mechanism? Can I live with it, laugh at it, or let it go? Suddenly, relationships, careers, and even parenting start to feel less like guesswork and more like navigating with a decent map.

And maybe that's the biggest takeaway. Self-discovery isn't about fixing what people can't stand about you. It's about finally seeing the design behind it all, the brilliance in the flaws, the lessons in the struggles, the humor in the contradictions. Because once you see yourself (and everyone else) clearly, you realize life isn't about changing people into something they're not. It's about working with the blueprint you've been given and laughing when the math doesn't add up exactly the way you expected.

If you want to see how Life Path numbers actually play out in real life, with real people, real quirks, and occasionally questionable decisions, come hang out with me on YouTube: @IHaveYourNumber. I share stories, patterns, and relatable examples that'll help anchor each Life Path in your brain (without needing flashcards or a vision board). Think of it as numerology with personality, and maybe more than a few ah-ha moments that make this whole "understanding humans" thing a little easier.

## Last thoughts:

**Life Path 1:** You were born to lead, innovate, and blaze trails no one else dares step on. Just remember, leadership isn't about bulldozing your way to the top, it's about inspiring others to walk beside you. Your independence is your superpower, but don't let it wall you off from love and collaboration. Keep charging forward, yes, but pause now and then to look back, wave, and make sure the people who adore you are still keeping up. Because trust me, they want to.

**Life Path 2:** Your gift is connection; you see people, you hear them, you smooth the edges that no one else even notices. Your intuition is a strength, not a liability. Learn to say 'no' with love, and you'll finally give yourself the same peace you've been giving everyone else. It isn't selfish to take care of your own needs; it's necessary. When you find that balance, you will be happier, calmer, and more able to bring your unique gifts to the world. You are not a grief concierge. You are a caring communicator. Stay in your lane, sweet soul.

**Life Path 3:** Your words, laughter, and ideas are medicine; don't waste them worrying about being taken seriously. You don't have to be perfect to be powerful. Let yourself play, tell your stories, and remember, the world needs your sparkle, not your silence. So, keep talking, keep dreaming, and when in doubt, throw in a punchline. Nine times out of ten, it will land perfectly. Learning how to read the emotions of others is a superpower in itself. Laughter is a gift, but true connection comes from listening and understanding what people need in the moment.

**Life Path 4:** Perfection builds walls, but flexibility builds bridges. Not every plan has to be perfect. The world won't end if you take a detour, laugh at the mess, or let yourself play once in a while. Your gift is stability, but your growth comes from remembering that life isn't only about holding it all together; sometimes it's about letting it fall into place on its own. I know it isn't your first choice, but if you stop pushing the river, you'll discover the river will calm right down and move into perfect flow.

**Life Path 5:** You're here for the ride, not the itinerary. Stop worrying about whether you'll ever "settle down," and just settle into being fully alive. Your gift is reminding the rest of us that freedom, curiosity, and joy aren't luxuries; they're necessities. So, keep exploring, keep laughing, and please, at least occasionally, text back.

"Remember, people respect honesty more than empty promises. If you can't commit to something, it's better to say so up front. Freedom isn't about avoiding commitments; it's about choosing the ones that matter and being honest about the ones you can't make." [1]

**Life Path 6:** Remember, the same heart that makes you a caregiver, healer, and fixer also deserves care, healing, and joy. Don't just pour yourself into everyone else's cup, save a little for your own. The world doesn't need you perfect; it needs you present. Love big, but love yourself just as much. Leadership isn't about controlling every detail. It's about empowering others, valuing their contributions, and fostering an environment where everyone can thrive and shine. By letting go of your need for perfection and embracing collaboration, you'll discover a better version of yourself.

---

[1] D.A. Mintaka, When Life Knocks You Off Your Happy, (California: Taking Flight Publishing, 2025), 27.

**Life Path 7:** You're the philosopher, the seeker, the one who always needs a little quiet to make sense of the noise. Just don't get so lost in your head that you forget to live in your body. Wisdom is beautiful, but so is a good laugh with friends, or, you know, remembering to eat lunch. Your gift is seeing truths that others miss, but your growth comes from sharing those truths without building walls around yourself. Don't hide, don't brood, come join us. The world needs your insight, but we also need your company.

**Life Path 8:** You're the powerhouse, the boss, the one who knows how to climb mountains and then buy the land around them. Just remember, not every hill is worth conquering, and not every battle is proof of your strength. Your drive is unmatched, but your soul expands when you balance achievement with generosity. Build your empire, yes, but don't forget to build relationships that last longer than the bottom line. Your legacy is measured in love just as much as it is in leadership.

**Life Path 9:** You're the memory keeper, the old soul, the one who feels the weight of the world and still insists on carrying extra bags for strangers. Your growth comes from remembering to include yourself in the circle of compassion. Learn that true memories are built from love, connection, and embracing the imperfect. Cherishing the present is more important than holding on to the past. Release the guilt, let go of what's already gone, and try to stop feeling like a victim. We are here to support you.

**Life Path 11:** Your value to the world is the way you light it up from the inside. You feel things deeply, you notice what others miss, and you're brave enough to share it. That mix of sensitivity and vision reminds people that life is bigger than the surface details, that meaning matters. You bring possibility to the table, and you inspire people to believe in more than what they can see. The world needs that reminder, and it needs you.

**Life Path 22:** Your value to the world is your ability to turn vision into reality. You remind people that ambition doesn't have to be cold, and practicality doesn't have to be boring. When you're aligned, your work becomes sacred, and the systems you create ripple out to help more people than you'll ever meet. The world leans on you to prove that lasting change is possible, and you deliver it one solid, determined step at a time.

**Life Path 33:** You have a unique way of blending heart, vision, and high standards into something the rest of us can actually live inside of. Yes, your standards can sting at times, but they're also what make life richer, more meaningful, and far more polished when you've had your say. You remind people that love isn't just a feeling, it's an action, a practice, and sometimes, a masterpiece in progress. The world is brighter, kinder, and sharper because you refuse to let it stay ordinary.

**Life Path 44:** Where others see limits, you see blueprints, and you remind people that structure doesn't have to be a cage; it can be freedom when designed with vision. Yes, your intensity can feel unyielding, but it's also what makes you the person others can trust when the storm hits. You teach us that discipline and intuition aren't opposites but partners, and that true power is not in controlling everything but in creating something that lasts. The world leans on your steadiness, even if it never says thank you out loud, and it's better, stronger, and more grounded because you are here.

**Life Path 55:** Your value to the world is your fearless refusal to play by the rules. Where others cling to the comfort of routine, you barge in and flip the table. You remind us that freedom is sacred, that change is inevitable, and that comfort zones are prisons disguised as cozy sweaters. Sure, your energy can be chaotic, and yes, people sometimes need to practice deep breathing to keep up with you, but you bring the spark that jolts the rest of us awake. You are the interrupter of stale traditions, the instigator of new paths, the one who pushes us to be braver than we thought we could be. The world needs your wildness because without it, we'd all stay stuck in old systems that don't work anymore. You are proof that disruption isn't destruction, it's the beginning of something brand new. And we are all the better for your efforts.

# Thank you

I'm truly grateful you took the time to read this book. Writing it has been a journey of passion, discovery, and dedication, and knowing that it has reached you means the world to me. If this book resonated with you, inspired you, or simply made you think, I would love to hear your thoughts. Leaving a review, no matter how short, makes an incredible difference. It not only helps other readers discover this book but also supports my vision of bringing more information like this into the world.

May you find the right words, the right timing, and the right understanding to make every relationship, especially the one with yourself, a little lighter, brighter, and easier to love. Your words have the power to uplift and encourage, just as I hope mine have done for you. Thank you for being a part of this journey.

With respect and gratitude,

Debra Zachau

9 781732 342668